Our selection of the city's best places to eat, drink and experience:

◎ **Sights**

✗ **Eating**

♟ **Drinking**

✪ **Entertainment**

🔒 **Shopping**

These symbols give you the vital information for each listing:

- ☎ Telephone Numbers
- ⊙ Opening Hours
- P Parking
- 🚭 Nonsmoking
- @ Internet Access
- 🛜 Wi-Fi Access
- ✔ Vegetarian Selection
- 📖 English-Language Menu
- 🚸 Family-Friendly
- 🐾 Pet-Friendly
- 🚌 Bus
- ⛴ Ferry
- Ⓜ Metro
- Ⓢ Subway
- ⊖ London Tube
- 🚋 Tram
- 🚆 Train

Find each listing quickly on maps for each neighbourhood:

Bar Hemingway

16 ♟ Map p233, B2

Legend has it that Hemi self, wielding a machine ate this timber-pan ered bar during showpiece is a en by Papa ar s.com; Hôtel Rit ⊙6.30pm-2a

6 ◎ Plac

Lonely Planet's Orlando & Walt Disney World® Resort

Lonely Planet Pocket Guides are designed to get you straight to the heart of the city.

Inside you'll find all the must-see sights, plus tips to make your visit to each one really memorable. We've split the city into easy-to-navigate regions and provided clear maps so you'll find your way around with ease. Our expert authors have searched out the best of the city: walks, food, nightlife and shopping, to name a few. Because you want to explore, our 'Local Life' pages will take you to some of the most exciting areas to experience the real Orlando and Walt Disney World® Resort.

And of course you'll find all the practical tips you need for a smooth trip: itineraries for short visits, how to get around, and how much to tip the guy who serves you a drink at the end of a long day's exploration.

It's your guarantee of a really great experience.

Our Promise

You can trust our travel information because Lonely Planet authors visit the places we write about, each and every edition. We never accept freebies for positive coverage, so you can rely on us to tell it like it is.

QuickStart Guide 7

Explore 21

Worth a Trip:

The Best 117

Orlando & Walt Disney World® Resort's Best …

Survival Guide 137

QuickStart Guide

Welcome to Orlando & Walt Disney World® Resort

Boost your adrenaline on a hair-raising ride, hop on the Hogwarts Express and meet Elsa and Anna from *Frozen*. In Orlando, the Theme Park Capital of the World, there's plenty to explore – from theme-park thrills to gardens and galleries – and you're set for the trip of a lifetime.

Dudley Do-Right's Ripsaw Falls (p66), Islands of Adventure
KAMIRA/SHUTTERSTOCK ©

Orlando & Walt Disney World® Resort
Top Sights

Magic Kingdom (p24)

Old-school Disney and Cinderella's castle.

Islands of Adventure (p64)
Over-the-top, honest-to-goodness fun.

Legoland (p114)

Indulge all your Lego dreams.

Epcot (p30)

Quirky take on the future.

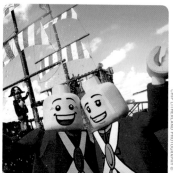

Disney's Animal Kingdom (p34)

Animal-themed park set in 'Africa.'

Charles Hosmer Morse Museum of American Art (p100)

Unique insight into Tiffany lamps.

OSCAR GARCES/AGE FOTOSTOCK ©

Universal Studios (p60)

Imaginative representations of favorite worlds.

Disney's Hollywood Studios (p38) Hollywood nostalgia and 21st-century energy.

Orlando & Walt Disney World® Resort
Local Life

Local experiences and hidden gems to help you uncover the real city

After checking off Orlando's top sights, seek out the craft cocktail bars, lakes lined with historic homes and indie live music that make up Orlando for locals. For vintage Disney, take the monorail to Magic Kingdom.

WILLIAM SHAKESPEARE MOSAIC BY SUZI K. EDWARDS / RICHARD CUMMINS/GETTY IMAGES ©

Loch Haven Park (p96)

☑ excellent museums ☑ beer-garden drinks

A Night Out in Downtown Orlando (p88)

☑ field-to-fork dining ☑ craft cocktails

Fresh & Wild in Winter Park (p102)

☑ canal cruises ☑ lakeside sculpture

Other great places to experience the city like a local:

Disney screenings and performances

Halloween Horror Nights (p70)

CityWalk (p76)

Restaurant Row (p83)

Enzian Theater (p108)

Orlando Farmers Market (p94)

Winter Park Farmers Market (p107)

Audubon Park (p129)

A Classic Day in Magic Kingdom (p42)

☑ iconic rides ☑ charming parades

Orlando & Walt Disney World® Resort
Day Planner

Day One

☀ Arrive in **Magic Kingdom** (p24) before the gates open, and watch the opening ceremony. March down Main Street to Fantasyland, and hop on Peter Pan's Flight and Seven Dwarfs Mine Train before the lines get long. Scurry over to Splash Mountain, zip across to Space Mountain, and finish your race to cover the biggies with the Pirates of Caribbean before the lines swell.

☀ Eat lunch with Minnie Mouse at **Chef Mickey's** (p42), take in Mickey's PhilharMagic and Monsters, Inc Laugh Floor, hit other rides, and watch the **Festival of Fantasy** (p28) parade. Wander the shops of Main St, USA and go to the FastPass+ kiosk to try for nighttime return-times for your favorite attractions.

☾ Leave the park and catch a boat to Disney's Grand Polynesian Resort for cocktails at **Tambu Lounge** (p54) and family-style kebabs at **'Ohana** (p50). After dinner, hop on the monorail back to Magic Kingdom, return to FastPass+ attractions and catch the **nighttime spectacular** (p25).

Day Two

☀ Be one of the first into **Epcot** (p30) and ride Soarin', Test Track and Spaceship Earth. Eat, drink and shop your way around the world at World Showcase, stopping for lunch at **La Cantina de San Angel** (p51) or try to make an advanced reservation at a table-service spot at World Showcase.

☀ Walk or take a boat to **Disney's Hollywood Studios** (p38). Ride Star Tours, Twilight Zone Tower of Terror and Rock 'n' Roller Coaster, and take in Beauty and the Beast – Live on Stage. You'll want to arrange FastPass+ reservations for these rides, if you can.

☾ Walk over to **Disney's BoardWalk** (p47) and wander along the waterfront. Head upstairs at the seaside inn for a drink at the **Belle Vue Room** (p53) and eat dinner at **Flying Fish** (p52). Catch a Disney bus, or drive, to Downtown Disney for **Cirque du Soleil La Nouba** (p55).

Short on time?
We've arranged Orlando & Walt Disney World® Resort's must-sees into these day-by-day itineraries to make sure you see the very best of the city in the time you have available.

Day Three

Head to **Universal Studios** (p60) when it opens, and go straight to **Wizarding World of Harry Potter – Diagon Alley** (p61); if you've spent the night at a Universal Orlando resort hotel, you can get into Harry Potter attractions one hour before the gates open to the public. Ride Escape from Gringotts then hop on the Hogwarts Express to **Hogsmeade** (p65) and take in the wand experience at Ollivanders.

Wander the shops of Hogsmeade, ride Dragon Challenge and have lunch at **Confisco Grille & Backwater Bar** (p72). Hit the rest of the roller coasters and water rides in **Islands of Adventure** (p64) before catching the Hogwarts Express back to explore Diagon Alley. Finish off with rides at Universal Studios and head out of the park.

Take a Universal resort boat over to Portofino Bay Hotel, and relax over a bowl of pasta and a glass of wine at **Mama Della's Ristorante** (p71).

Day Four

Start the day early and drive to **Wekiwa Springs State Park** (p136). Rent a canoe and paddle past alligators and turtles on the quiet waters of Wekiva River, take a hike along a woodland trail, and tube down the creek at **Kelly Park** (p136).

Head to historic Winter Park (p98) for the afternoon. Don't miss the **Charles Hosmer Morse Museum of American Art** (p100), home to the world's largest collection of Louis Comfort Tiffany art. Rent a bike from **Breakaway Bikes** (p143) and take a spin around the neighborhoods, or hop on an intimate one-hour boat tour. Later, stroll down Park Ave, stopping for a Napoleon at **Croissant Gourmet** (p102).

Sip a self-serve wine flight at **Wine Room** (p108), indulge in some of the city's best field-to-fork dining at **Luma on Park** (p107) or **Prato** (p106; try to snag a sidewalk table), and take in a movie at the indie **Enzian Theater** (p108).

Need to Know

For more information,
see Survival Guide (p137)

Currency
US dollar ($)

Language
English

Visas
Visitors from Canada, the UK, Australia,
New Zealand, Japan and many EU
countries don't need visas for stays of less
than 90 days. Other nations see http://
travel.state.gov.

Money
ATMs widely available. Credit cards
accepted at most hotels, restaurants and
shops.

Mobile Phones
Foreign phones that operate on tri- or
quad-band frequencies will work in the
USA. Otherwise, purchase inexpensive cell
phones with a pay-as-you-go plan here.

Time
Eastern Standard Time (GMT/UTC minus
five hours)

Plugs & Adaptors
AC 110V is standard; buy adapters to run most
non-US electronics.

Tipping
Airport and hotel porters $2 per bag. Bartenders
15% to 20% per round (minimum per drink
$1). Hotel maids $2 to $4 per night. Restaurant
servers 15% to 20%. Taxi drivers 10% to 15%.

1 Before You Go

Your Daily Budget

Budget: Less than $200
▶ Walt Disney World® value resort for four
people: $110
▶ Self-catering and cheap eats: $40–60
▶ Seven-day bus pass: $16

Midrange: $200–400
▶ Theme-park accommodation for four: $200
▶ Multiday theme-park ticket: $50–120
▶ Car rental per week: $300–400

Top end: More than $400
▶ Luxury or easy theme-park access accommodation for four: $400-plus
▶ Theater ticket: $40–80
▶ Themed Disney dining or top-end
restaurant: $90–160

Useful Websites
Lonely Planet (www.lonelyplanet.com/usa/
florida/orlando)

Walt Disney World® (www.disneyworld.
disney.go.com)

Universal Orlando Resort (www.universal
orlando.com)

Orlando Visitor Center (www.visitorlando.
com)

Advance Planning

Three months before Snag a table at
Disney character, themed and high-end
restaurants.

Two months before Book your hotel,
purchase theme-park tickets and reserve
Disney FastPass+ attractions (if not staying on-site, reserve 30 days in advance).

Three weeks before Buy theater tickets.

② Arriving in Orlando

Orlando International Airport (MCO; ☎407-825-8463; www.orlandoairports.net; 1 Jeff Fuqua Blvd) handles more passengers than any other airport in Florida. It serves Walt Disney World®, the Space Coast and the Orlando area.

Orlando Sanford International Airport (☎407-585-4000; www.orlandosanford airport.com; 1200 Red Cleveland Blvd) is a small airport 30 minutes north of downtown Orlando and 45 minutes north of Walt Disney World®.

Greyhound (☎407-292-3424; www.grey hound.com; 555 N John Young Pkwy) serves numerous cities from Orlando.

Amtrak (www.amtrak.com; 1400 Sligh Blvd) offers daily trains south to Miami (from $46) and north to New York City (from $144).

To & From the Airports

If you are flying into Orlando International Airport and are staying at a Walt Disney World® Resort, arrange in advance for com-plimentary luxury bus transportation to and from the airport through **Disney's Magical Express** (☎866-599-0951; www.disney world.disney.go.com).

Orlando Airport Towncar (☎800-532-8563, www.orlandoairporttowncar.com) Greets you at baggage claim at Orlando International and Orlando Sanford Airports. Transport to Walt Disney World® costs one way/return $60/120 for one to four people in a town car; $85/170 for one to six people in an SUV. It's about $20 less for transport to Universal Orlando Resort.

Legacy Towncar of Orlando (☎888-939-8227; www.legacytowncar.com) Prices include a 20-minute grocery-store stop. Round trip to Universal, Walt Disney World® or International Dr costs $120 for a town car seating up to four people; $155 for a five- to nine-person van.

③ Getting Around

You'll need a car to explore beyond the theme parks and International Dr.

🚗 Car Rental

Both Orlando International and Orlando Sanford International Airports, Walt Disney World® and many hotels have car-rental agencies. Disney's Car Care Center and the Walt Disney World® Dolphin Hotel offer Alamo and National car rentals, and there are rental-car desks at Universal Orlando Resort Hotels.

Theme Park Transportation

Both Walt Disney World® Resort and Uni-versal Orlando Resort's complimentary bus and boat transportation link their hotels, entertainment districts and theme parks, and three Disney monorail routes connect Magic Kingdom, Epcot, select Disney resort hotels and the Transportation & Ticket Center. You don't need theme-park admission to use the resort transportation, and you don't need to be a guest at a Disney or Universal hotel.

🚕 Taxi

Cabs sit outside the theme parks, Disney Springs, resorts and other tourist centers; oth-erwise you'll need to call to arrange a pickup.

🚃 Trolleybus

I-Ride Trolley (p143) services International Dr, from south of SeaWorld north to the Universal Orlando Resort area. Exact change is required.

🚆 Train

SunRail (www.sunrail.com), Orlando's com-muter rail train, runs north–south. It doesn't stop at or near any theme parks. Amtrak serves Downtown, Winter Park, Kissimmee and Winter Haven (home to Legoland).

🚌 Bus

Orlando's free Lymmo (p87) circles the down-town area. Lynx (p141) buses cover greater Orlando but service is limited after 8pm.

Orlando & Walt Disney World® Resort
Regions

International Drive (p78)
Orlando's tourist hub, filled with restaurants, bars, stores and sights.

Walt Disney World® Resort (p22)
With 40-sq-miles of theme parks, water parks, golf courses, entertainment districts and dozens of hotels, it's a world of Mickey.

👁 Top Sights

Magic Kingdom

Disney's Hollywood Studios

Epcot

Disney's Animal Kingdom

Magic Kingdom

Disney's Animal Kingdom

Epcot

Disney's Hollywood Studios

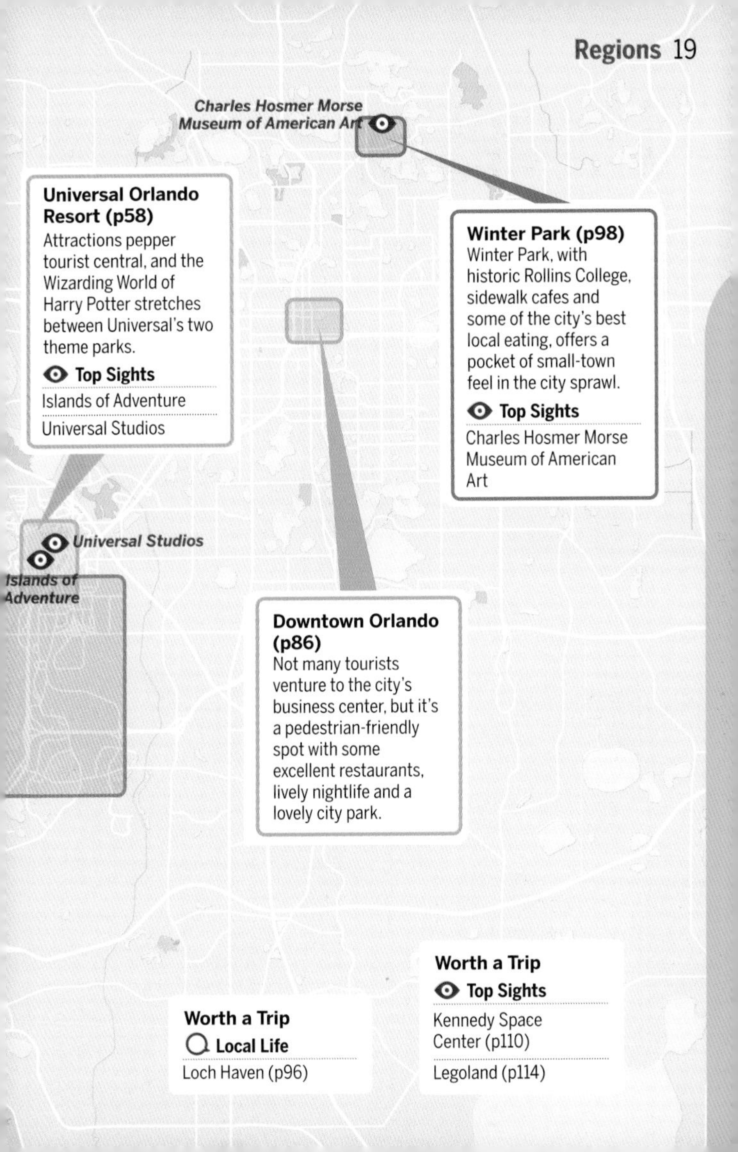

Charles Hosmer Morse
Museum of American Art ◉

Universal Orlando Resort (p58)

Attractions pepper tourist central, and the Wizarding World of Harry Potter stretches between Universal's two theme parks.

◉ Top Sights

Islands of Adventure

Universal Studios

Winter Park (p98)

Winter Park, with historic Rollins College, sidewalk cafes and some of the city's best local eating, offers a pocket of small-town feel in the city sprawl.

◉ Top Sights

Charles Hosmer Morse Museum of American Art

◉ Universal Studios

◉ Islands of Adventure

Downtown Orlando (p86)

Not many tourists venture to the city's business center, but it's a pedestrian-friendly spot with some excellent restaurants, lively nightlife and a lovely city park.

Worth a Trip
◉ Top Sights

Kennedy Space Center (p110)

Legoland (p114)

Worth a Trip
○ Local Life

Loch Haven (p96)

Explore

Orlando & Walt Disney World® Resort

Worth a Trip

World Showcase (p32), Epcot
APHOTOSTORY/SHUTTERSTOCK ©

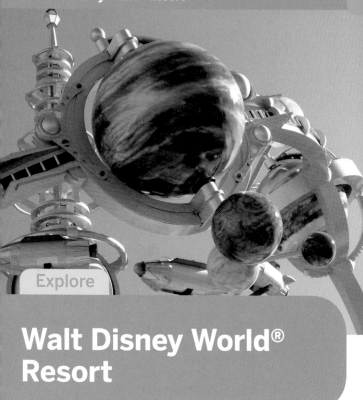

Explore

Walt Disney World® Resort

Walt Disney World® Resort attracts millions of people from around the globe every year. Its theme parks, filled with rides, live shows, 3D movies and parades, transport visitors into a land of princesses and pirates, monsters and magic. But it's not just theme parks. Like Walt himself imagined, it's an entire, self-contained *world* of Mickey.

Theme Parks, Water Parks & More

Walt Disney World® covers more than 40 sq miles and includes four separate (walled) theme parks, two water parks and some golf courses, all connected by a complicated system of monorail, boat and bus, and intersected by highways and roads. Rides, character interactions, movies and shows are spread out among the parks, resort hotels, and entertainment districts.

Magic Kingdom (p24) Low on thrills and high on nostalgia, with Cinderella's Castle and nightly fireworks.

Epcot (p30) A handful of rides on one side, country-based food, shopping and attractions on the other.

Disney's Animal Kingdom (p34) Part zoo and part county fair, with a heavy dusting of Disney-styled Africa.

Hollywood Studios (p38) Movie-based attractions and Pixar characters.

Typhoon Lagoon (p46) Water park particularly excellent for families.

Blizzard Beach (p46) Water park with high-speed twists and turns.

Disney's BoardWalk (p47) Intimate waterfront area with a handful of shops, restaurants and entertainment; no admission fee.

Disney Springs (p54) Recently revamped area devoted to shops, bars and entertainment; no admission fee.

👁 Top Sights

🔍 Local Life

❤ Best of Walt Disney World® Resort

Themed Dining

Performing Arts

Getting There

🚗 **Car** Take I-4 to well-signed exits 64, 65 or 67. See p143 for important parking information.

🚌 **Bus** Lynx 50 connects the downtown central station to Disney's Transportation & Ticket Center (TTC) and Disney Springs. Bus 56 runs along Hwy 192, between Kissimmee and TTC. From there, you can connect to any theme park or hotel.

Top Sights
Magic Kingdom

Walt Disney World®'s Magic Kingdom is the quintessential old-school Disney with classic rides and Cinderella's Castle and Tinker Bell (although these days, there are recent additions such as Elsa and Merida). Aimed at littlies, you won't find many high-speed thrills or state-of-the-art rides here. Things move a little more gently. This kingdom is about magic and fantasy and the characters, and the lands they live in are so real, you're guaranteed to lose yourself, if only for the day.

👁 Map p44, E1

📞 407-939-5277

www.disneyworld.disney.go.com

1180 Seven Seas Dr, Walt Disney World®

$100-119, prices vary daily

🕒 9am-11pm, hours vary

Nighttime Spectacular, Cinderella's Castle

Fantasyland

Quintessential Disney and home to the sweet Winnie-the-Pooh, Peter Pan, Dumbo, Ariel and Snow White–themed rides, **Fantasyland** (⊙9am-9pm, hours vary) is the highlight of any Disney trip for both the eight-and-under crowd and grown-ups looking for a nostalgic taste of classic Disney. Keep an eye out for Cinderella, Mary Poppins, Alice in Wonderland and other favorites hanging out throughout Fantasyland, or hop in line to see princesses at **Fairy Tale Hall** (FastPass+) and Mickey, Minnie, Goofy and Donald at the circus-themed **Pete's Silly Sideshow** (no FastPass+).

Nighttime Spectacular

More than just a fireworks display, the Nighttime Spectacular captures the essence of Disney magic in an extravaganza of light and music, storytelling and fireworks, set around Cinderella's Castle. It changes name every couple of years, it seems, with new shows and effects. Its most recent incarnation, launched with a bang (sorry) in 2017 is 'Happily Ever After'.

Mickey's PhilharMagic

Without a doubt the best 3D show in Disney, Mickey's PhilharMagic takes Donald Duck on a whimsical adventure through classic Disney movies. Ride with him through the streets of Morocco on Aladdin's carpet and feel the champagne on your face when it pops open during Beauty and the Beast's **Be Our Guest** (☎407-939-3463; ⊙8am-10:30am, 11am-2.30pm & 4-10pm, hours vary).

Enchanted Tales with Belle

This Character Spot inside Fantasyland doubles as one of the park's sweetest interactive experiences. Groups of about 20 at a time enter Maurice's cottage, where a magic mirror sparkles and turns into a doorway leading to the Beast's castle.

☑ Top Tips

▶ Best attractions to use as your three Fast-Pass+ selections are Peter Pan's Flight, Big Thunder Mountain Railroad, Splash Mountain, Space Mountain, Seven Dwarf's Mine Train, Princess Fairytale Hall and Enchanted Tales with Belle; or hit them when the park gates open.

▶ It's a Small World, Mickey's PhilharMagic, and Monsters, Inc Laugh Floor are air-conditioned and have short waits.

✗ Take a Break

Get an ice-cream sandwich from **Sleepy Hollow** (snacks $6-9; ⊙9am-park closing) and eat with castle views. For java with a kick, your only option is the Starbucks at **Main Street Bakery** (items $5-10; ⊙9am-park closing). Take your coffee left out the door to the corner and head left down the little side street; it's usually quiet and uncrowded, and there are a few tables.

From here, it's a combination of an interactive experience and a character greeting, in which selected guests act out Beauty and the Beast for Belle herself.

Seven Dwarfs Mine Train
A marvelously smooth, family-friendly coaster, this 2014 Disney newbie replaced the vintage Snow White's Scary Adventure as Fantasyland's cornerstone princess-themed ride. Ride through the mine, past Grumpy, Happy and the others heaving their picks and singing 'Heigh Ho, Heigh Ho,' zip around and sideways, and end at the dwarfs' cottage.

Meet Gaston
Outside Gaston's Tavern (p53), and next to the fountain sculpture of Gaston, is Gaston himself. Everyone from little ones clutching autograph books to grandma and grandpa line up for photos with the arrogant brute. This one is a regular Character Spot, but mentioned because it's particularly entertaining – he jokes and banters and struts, in full character, and it's great fun to watch.

Frontierland
Frontierland (⊘9am-9pm, hours var) is Wild West Disney-style. **Splash Mountain** depicts the misadventures of Brer Rabbit, Brer Bear and Brer Fox, complete with chatty frogs, singing

---

Understand
Magic Kingdom
- -

When most people think of Walt Disney World®, they're thinking of the Magic Kingdom, which is just one of the four theme parks. At its core is Cinderella's Castle, the iconic image (this over-used phrase is used correctly here) of the television show. Remember when Tinker Bell dashed across the screen as fireworks burst across the castle turrets?

Paths from the castle lead to the four 'lands,' as well as two other areas:

Fantasyland (p25) The most nostalgic area, especially loved by littlies.

Tomorrowland (p28) A Jetsons-inspired peek into the future; home to Space Mountain.

Adventureland (p27) Pirates and jungles.

Frontierland (p26) Wild West.

Liberty Square (p27) Home to Haunted Mansion.

Main Street, USA (p46) Souvenir browsing in old-timey, small-town USA.

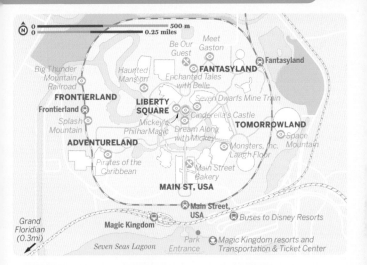

ducks and other critters. The 40mph drop into the river makes for one of the biggest thrills in the park, and you will get very wet! With no steep drops or loop-dee-loops, mild **Big Thunder Mountain Railroad** coaster is a great choice for little ones.

Pirates of the Caribbean

Adventureland (⊘9am-9pm, hours vary) is filled with pirates and jungles, magic carpets and tree houses, whimsical and silly representations of the exotic locales from storybooks and imagination. Don't miss **Pirates of the Caribbean** – the slow-moving boat through the dark and shadowy world of pirates remains one of the most popular attractions at Disney.

Haunted Mansion

The ramblin' 19th-century mansion houses **Haunted Mansion**, another classic favorite piece of low-on-thrill and high-on-silly fun, and the only real ride in **Liberty Square** (⊘9am-9pm, hours vary). Cruise slowly past the haunted dining room, where apparitions dance across the stony floor, but beware of those hitchhiking ghosts – don't be surprised if they jump into your car uninvited. While mostly it's lighthearted ghosty goofiness, kids may be frightened by spooky pre-ride dramatics.

Space Mountain

Clack, clack, clack...and zoom, you blast off into the darkness of space, surrounded by stars and asteroids, zipping up and around through the galaxy. Compared to modern coasters, this one is relatively mild, but it's a don't miss Disney classic with spectacular visual effects.

Monsters, Inc Laugh Floor

In the 2001 movie *Monsters, Inc,* Sully and Mike Wazowski and their lovable monster friends must harness human screams; in this interactive, live comedy show, the premise is that they must now harness laughter. A screen projects characters from the movie, each doing a stand-up comedy routine that surprises audience members by unexpectedly incorporating them.

Festival of Fantasy

Disney's daytime **parade** (⏱morning & afternoon daily, hours vary) features elaborate floats, beguiling costumes, marvelously choreographed dancing and, of course, favorite Disney characters, from Peter Pan and Sleeping Beauty to contemporary favorites like Anna, Elsa and Merida. Acrobats swing wildly and magnificent *Under the Sea* creatures shimmer and shake around Ariel, who calmly brushes her long red locks with a 'dinglehopper.'

Scavenger Hunt with Merlin

Sorcerers of the Magic Kingdom is a wildly popular, self-paced treasure-hunt-styled experience in which participants join Merlin in his efforts to find and defeat Disney villains. Players receive a key card that activates hidden game portals throughout Magic Kingdom, as well as a map and spell cards used to cast spells at these portals. Stop by the firehouse by the front entrance on Main Street, USA, or behind the Christmas shop in Liberty Square to sign up. Free with theme park admission.

Mickey's Royal Friendship Faire

Due to start at the time of research, another of Magic Kingdom's performance wows, with Mickey and a strange old mix of old friends and 'new': Goofy, Tiana and friends, Donald Duck, and even Olaf, Anna and Elsa. We are promised dance, special effects and musical scores. There will be several shows a day – check your Times Guide for times.

Understand

Top Tips for a Successful Disney Vacation

Disney expectations run high, and the reality of things can be disappointing. Long waits, and getting jostled and tugged through crowds and lines, can leave the kids, and you, exhausted. There are two ways to do this. The first is to plan ahead with scrupulous attention to detail. Make dinner reservations, plan when to go where based on parade and show schedules, decide in advance what attractions to tackle once you're there and reserve FastPass+ selections. Here are some simple tips:

Buy tickets that cover more days than you think you'll need It's less expensive per day, and it gives the freedom for downtime in the pool or at low-key attractions beyond theme-park gates.

Take Advantage of My Disney Experience Download the Disney App 'My Disney Experience' and reserve your three daily FastPass+ attractions in advance.

Stock up on snacks Even if it's nothing more than some snack packets and bananas, you'll save the irritation of waiting in line for bad, overpriced food. Or, to avoid the lines, buy a sandwich early on the way in and have a picnic at your leisure.

Arrive at the park at least 30 minutes before gates open Don't window shop or dawdle – just march quickly to the rides and then kick back for the afternoon. Factor in the time to get here from the Transportation & Ticket Center (this can take up to an hour).

Program Disney Dining into your cell phone While you'll want to make some plans well in advance, once you have a sense of where you'll be at meal time, call ☎407-939-3463 to make reservations at table-service restaurants.

Transport and accommodation When booking accommodation it's worth considering your transport options. All Disney resorts offer bus transportation, but those offering boat and monorail transportation are far more convenient (and, except for camping at Fort Wilderness, more expensive).

Go with the flow This is about managing expectations. If you build up the idea that your child will definitely hug Belle in a so-called 'character meet,' only to see the line is ridiculous, then recalibrate. Suggest initially that you're going to spot, rather than visit, a character. Believe us, you'll end up spotting them in parades or by chance.

Top Sights
Epcot

An acronym for 'Experimental Prototype Community of Tomorrow', Epcot was Disney's vision of a high-tech city when it opened in 1982. It's divided into two halves: Future World, with rides and interactive exhibits, and World Showcase (p32), providing an interesting toe-dip into the cultures of 11 countries. Epcot is much more soothingly low-key than other parks, and it has some of the best food and shopping.

👁 Map p44, C5

☎ 407-939-5277

www.disneyworld.disney.
go.com

200 Epcot Center Dr,
Walt Disney World®

$100-119, prices vary
daily

🕑 11am-9pm, hours vary

Spaceship Earth

Soarin' Around the World

Soar up and down, hover and accelerate as the giant screen in front of you takes you over and around the globe. We don't want to give too much away, suffice to say that this **ride** (Future World; ⊘9am-6pm, hours vary) is an extraordinarily visceral experience as aroma effects blast the smells of the earth at you as you ride (such as the elephants and grasses of Africa). Ask for a front-row seat; feet dangling in front of you can ruin the effect. Those who have severe motion sickness might find the images a little unsettling.

IllumiNations: Reflections of Earth

Epcot's **night show** (⊘nightly, hours vary) incorporates fireworks, elaborate light theatrics and dramatic music to create a fiery narrative of the earth's history, beginning with 'the earth is born.' It centers around a massive globe illuminated with LED lights in the middle of World Showcase Lagoon – find a spot at least an hour early.

Test Track

Board a car on **Test Track** (Future World; ⊘9am-6pm, hours vary) and ride through heat, cold, speed, braking and crash tests – at one point a huge semi with blinding lights heads right for you, its horn blaring. When testing the acceleration, the car speeds up to 60mph within a very short distance, but there are few turns and no ups and downs like a roller coaster.

Spaceship Earth

Inside what people joke is a giant golf ball landmark at the front entrance, **Spaceship Earth** (Future World; ⊘9am-6pm, hours vary) is a bizarre, kitschy slow-moving ride past animatronic

☑ Top Tips

▶ Best attractions to use as your three Fast-Pass+ selections are Frozen, Soarin' Around the World and Test Track, as wait times can be painfully long. Alternatively, hit them when the park gates open.

▶ To get here from Magic Kingdom, take a monorail to the Transportation & Ticket Center and transfer to the Epcot monorail; from Disney's Hollywood Studios and Epcot hotels, hop on a boat or walk the 15 minutes along the water.

✕ Take a Break

Head to Mexico for a taco from Cantina de San Angel (p51) and sit on the waterfront terrace.

scenes depicting the history of communication from cave painting to computers. Yes, it sounds boring, and yes, it sounds weird. But it's surprisingly funny and a cult favorite. In recent years they've tried to modernize it with an interactive questionnaire about your travel interests, but we like the retro aspects better.

The Seas with Nemo & Friends

In the style of the Winnie-the-Pooh and Peter Pan rides in Magic Kingdom, this sweet **jaunt** (Future World; ⊙9am-6pm, hours vary) in a clam shell takes you through the seas with Nemo. While it doesn't follow the story line, you'll see Dory, Mr Ray and Bruce the shark, and it ends at a gigantic saltwater aquarium filled with real critters from Nemo's sea.

Turtle Talk with Crush

A small blue room with a large movie screen features *Finding Nemo's* Crush, and kids gather to talk face-to-face with the famous turtle. He chats with the children staring up at him, taking questions from the 'dude in the dark-blue shell' and cracking jokes about how sea grass gives him the bubbles. Dory shows up and gets squished against the screen by the whale, and there's plenty of silliness and giggling.

Understand

World Showcase

- -

Without the emphasis on roller coasters and adrenaline, things run a bit slower here, with a bit less va-voom than in the rest of Disney World®. Slow down and enjoy the ambience. Sure, this is quite a sanitized stereotypical vision of the world and its future, but so what? It's still a theme park.

The best way to experience the **World Showcase** (⊙9am-6pm, hours vary) is to simply wander as the mood moves you, poking through stores and restaurants, and catching what amounts to Bureau of Tourism promotional films and gentle rides through some of the countries. Donald Duck and his comrades take you through Mexico in the **Gran Fiesta Tour Starring the Three Caballeros**, and the **American Adventure** show features animatronic figures presenting a simplified interpretation of US history. The featured countries from left to right around the water are Mexico, Norway, China, Germany, Italy, USA, Japan, Morocco, France, the UK and Canada.

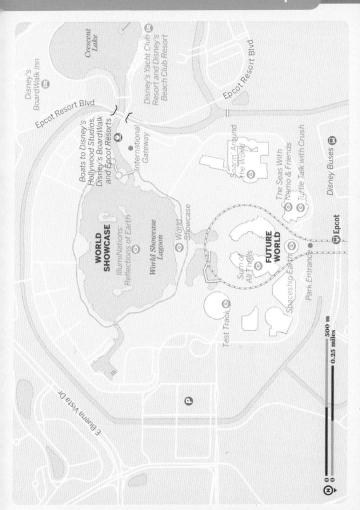

Cresent Lake

Disney's BoardWalk Inn

Disney's Yacht Club Resort and Disney's Beach Club Resort

Epcot Resort Blvd

Epcot Resort Blvd

Boats to Disney's Hollywood Studios, Disney's BoardWalk and Epcot Resorts

International Gateway

Soarin' Around the World

The Seas With Nemo & Friends

Turtle Talk with Crush

Disney Buses

WORLD SHOWCASE

IllumiNations: Reflections of Earth

World Showcase Lagoon

World Showcase

FUTURE WORLD

Sum of All Thrills

Epcot

Park Entrance

Spaceship Earth

Test Track

E Buena Vista Dr

500 m

0.25 miles

Top Sights
Disney's Animal Kingdom

A pleasant change from the 'fantastical fairy' elements of the rest of Disney, Animal Kingdom attempts to introduce some reality through animals in a natural zoo environment. But this is Disney, after all. It throws in a melange of carnival and Disney characters in a setting of Africa, with magical elements (especially with the recent introduction of The World of Avatar). It's the most relaxing, and shaded, of the Disney experiences.

◉ Map p44, A6

☎ 407-939-5277

www.disneyworld.disney.go.com

2101 Osceola Pkwy, Walt Disney World®

$100-119, prices vary daily

🕓 9am-7pm, hours vary

Expedition Everest

Finding Nemo: the Musical

Arguably the best show at Walt Disney World® Resort, **Finding Nemo: the Musical** (⊘several shows daily) is a sophisticated 40-minute musical theater performance that features massive and elaborate puppets on stage and down the aisles, incredible set design and great acting. The music was composed by Robert Lopez and Kirsten Anderson-Lopez, who also wrote Frozen's Academy Award–winning 'Let It Go', and the spectacular puppets were created by Michael Curry, the creative and artistic force behind the puppets in Broadway's *The Lion King*.

Kilimanjaro Safaris

Board a jeep and ride through the African Savannah, pausing to look at zebras, lions, giraffes, alligators and more, all seemingly roaming free. Sometimes you'll have to wait to let an animal cross the road, and if you're lucky you'll see babies or some raucous activity. These are not classic Disney auto-animatronic creatures. These are real, live animals and you are on safari in Africa.

DINOSAUR

A dinosaur-inspired multisensory simulated ride into prehistoric jungles takes you through the darkness and past all kinds of animatronic beasts of the Mesozoic. Be warned – there's plenty of mayhem and panic, and you barely escape the menacing Carnotaurus and the crash of the meteor.

Expedition Everest

Wait in a reconstructed Nepalese village, made to make you feel like you are indeed about to take a train to the top of Mt Everest. A mini museum

☑ Top Tips

▶ Best attractions to use as your three FastPass+ selections are Kilimanjaro Safaris, Expedition Everest, DINOSAUR and Kali River Rapids. Or, hit them when the park gates open.

▶ Check out the rides at Pandora – The World of Avatar.

▶ Disney buses stop at Animal Kingdom, but the ride here can be up to 45 minutes or longer. There is parking just outside the park gates.

✕ Take a Break

Grab a cold beer at the thatch-roofed Dawa Bar (p54) in Harambe Village or head to the **Yak and Yeti** (mains $15-29; ⊘11am–park closing) in Asia for surprisingly good Asian fare. Short trails around Animal Kingdom's Discovery Island lead to quiet spots along the water, where the benches make a great place to relax with a snack. Keep an eye out for tortoises and monkeys.

focusing on the mountain's climbers contains copious evidence of a mysterious mountain creature, but you pay no attention. Like so much of Disney, the ride is as much about the narrative shtick as the ride, but this coaster faces the Yeti, zips backwards and zooms around turns.

Festival of the Lion King

This theater-in-the-round combines larger-than-life puppets, parade- and circus-inspired choreography, dramatic costumes and audience interaction to create a high-energy, eye-candy musical celebration of *The Lion King*. It doesn't follow the story line, but it incorporates the characters and songs. Be prepared to belt out warthog, giraffe, lion and elephant noises!

Kali River Rapids

Wind through the rain forest, down gentle drops and past waterfalls on a 12-person circular raft. Folks on the sidelines squirt water at the boats as they bounce down the rapids, and it's a sure-fire guarantee that you'll get absolutely dripping-wet, wring-out-the-water-from-your-shirt soaked. Lock up phones and valuables in the free lockers.

Flights of Wonder

Sure, some complain that it's just a bird show, and yes, there's plenty of cheesy dialog, but the macaws, cockatoos and parrots are spectacular as they zoom around over your head. The bantering and audience interaction offer silly fun, and it's a great place to sit and relax out of the sun.

Rivers of Light

This sound-and-light **show** (⏱7:15pm, 8:30pm, times vary) over water focuses on the theme of nature. It presents stunning effects from fireflies flitting across the lake to 'spirit forms' of the world's animals and is a fitting end to this little, tropical, ever-so controlled and very animal sanitized 'paradise'. Reserve ahead with your Fastpass+.

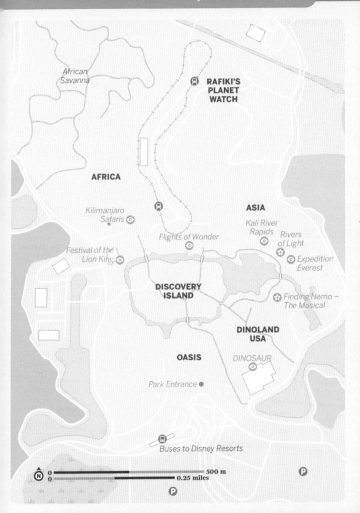

African Savanna

RAFIKI'S PLANET WATCH

AFRICA

ASIA

Kilimanjaro Safaris

Kali River Rapids

Rivers of Light

Flights of Wonder

Expedition Everest

Festival of the Lion King

DISCOVERY ISLAND

Finding Nemo – The Musical

DINOLAND USA

OASIS

DINOSAUR

Park Entrance

Buses to Disney Resorts

N
0   500 m
0   0.25 miles

Top Sights
Disney's Hollywood Studios

Hollywood Studios is meant to conjure the heydays of Hollywood but most of the attractions find their inspiration from unabashed 21st-century energy. Future young Jedi line up daily to prepare for *Star Wars* Jedi Training and *Frozen* souvenirs line store shelves while screams from the Tower of Terror echo through the park. Several Disney jewels, including some of the best thrills and princess shows, sparkle through the filler and fluff.

👁 Map p44, C5

📞 407-939-5277

www.disneyworld.disney.go.com

351 S Studio Dr, Walt Disney World®

$100-119, prices vary daily

🕑 9am-10pm, hours vary

Star Tours: The Adventures Continue

Twilight Zone Tower of Terror

The preride spiel explains how the building, once a bustling Hollywood hotel, came to be so ramshackle and empty, and then, Rod Serling invites you into...The Twilight Zone. Enter an elevator and slowly climb up through the eerie old hotel, past the lurking ghosts. Clatter, clatter, clatter, until suddenly and without warning the elevator free falls. Clatter up, crash down, again and again, all in total darkness.

Star Tours: The Adventures Continue

Don 3D glasses and hop onto a Starspeeder 1000 for this simulated voyage into the *Star Wars* galaxy. You zoom through the alien desert terrain in a desperate effort to escape Darth Vader, meet R2D2 and other *Star Wars* folk, and return (phew!) to the Alliance base. There are more than 50 story lines, so you'll have a new ride each time.

Beauty and the Beast – Live on Stage

A simple and sweet outdoor performance with elaborate costumes, choreography and stage design that follows the story line, incorporates the classic songs, and doesn't fall back on any special effects or crazy shenanigans. The 25-minute show opened in 1991 on the same day as the movie was released, and it hasn't changed much since.

Sci-Fi Dine-In Theater

In typical Disney style, eating is rarely just about eating. Though officially a **restaurant** (mains $15-24; ⊙11am-8:30pm), the tables are cut into mock convertibles, stars twinkle in the darkness and kitschy old-school science fiction films run continuously on the massive screen. There's a strange satisfaction in eating burgers in a 1950s drive-in

---

☑ Top Tips

▸ *Star Wars* fanatics should hit Star Tours when the gates open – you'll be able to ride several times in a row without a long line and every ride is different.

▸ Best attractions to use as your three FastPass+ selections are Toy Story Mania, Rock 'n' Roller Coaster, Twilight Zone Tower of Terror and Star Tours; wait times at these rides can be painfully long. Alternatively, hit them when the park gates open.

▸ Don't waste a Fast-Pass+ on Disney Junior or Muppet Vision 3D since they have the shortest waits.

✗ Take a Break

People-watch over a martini flight on the outdoor terrace at Hollywood Brown Derby Lounge (p51); at the end of the day, it's a short hop on a Disney boat to Disney Boardwalk's Belle Vue Room (p53).

theater, and who doesn't want a glow-in-the-dark Tinker Bell perched on their drink?

Star Wars Launch Bay

At one of Hollywood's newest additions, you can become fully immersed into the world of *Star Wars* through movie props, meet and greets with characters, from Chewbacca to Kylo Ren, plus a movie revealing a behind-the-scenes look at the creation of the *Star Wars* extravaganza.

Jedi Training: Trials of the Temple

A group of children don brown robes, pledge the sacred Jedi oath and grab a light saber for on-stage **training** (⏱from 9am, up to 15 times a day) by a Jedi Master. But it's first-come, first-served, so get to Hollywood Studios when gates open and line up at the Indiana Adventure Outpost, near the 50's Prime Time Café, to sign up for one of the many classes held throughout the day. For children age four to 12.

Star Wars: A Galactic Spectacular

Hollywood Studios' nighttime fireworks show features every pyrotechnic, laser and light that shines and bursts to none other than a – da da da daaaaaa da! – *Star Wars* theme and soundtrack.

Rock 'n' Roller Coaster Starring Aerosmith

The rather odd schtick is that you're hurrying off in a limo to catch the Aerosmith concert. 'Dude (Looks Like a Lady)', or another Aerosmith song, cranks through headrest speakers as the coaster twists and turns in darkness, but there are no steep drops that send your belly through your mouth.

50's Prime Time Café

Another masterfully designed trip into the past, this is a **restaurant** (mains $17-23; ⏱11am–park closing) set in grandma's kitchen c 1950. TVs throughout the kitchen screen black-and-white sitcoms like *Father Knows Best* and the original *Mickey Mouse Club* and wait staff treat you like family. Classic Disney silliness, kitschy interaction and huge plates of Americana comfort food.

Voyage of the Little Mermaid

Fluorescent sea critters (handled by puppeteers swathed in black) pop out in a brilliant flash of color, bubbles descend from the ceiling to complete the underwater effect, and Ariel croons classic songs from the film. Prepare to be splashed as you go 'underwater' so keep cameras and cell phones tucked away. It's a great live theater performance, but it doesn't follow the story line and we wish it were longer.

One Man's Dream

This walk through Disney history features all kinds of Walt Disney

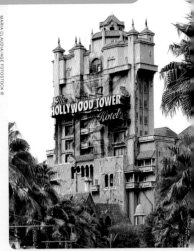

MARIA CLAUDIA/AGE FOTOSTOCK ©

Twilight Zone Tower of Terror (p39)

memorabilia and interesting tidbits about the man, his vision and his legacy. It's a bit of a grab-bag, with vintage toys, Walt's second-grade desk, original models of Disney attractions and more, arranged chronologically. The theater plays 'sneak peaks' of upcoming releases in unashamed, in-your-face Disney style.

Toy Story Midway Mania!

Hop onto spinning cars and cruise past carnival-inspired games, while shooting at virtual eggs, pies and suction darts trying to rack up points. You compete with your seatmate, and there are all kinds of *Toy Story*–themed, 4D special effects.

Local Life
A Classic Day in Magic Kingdom

Magic Kingdom, the oldest theme park at Walt Disney World® Resort, is a must for anyone looking for the nostalgic charm of vintage Disney movies, rides and characters. For this Classic Disney Day, you'll need admission to Magic Kingdom, and, if you can, FastPass+ reservations for Space Mountain, Splash Mountain, Pirates of the Caribbean, Enchanted Tales with Belle and Seven Dwarfs Train.

❶ Breakfast with Mickey

Nothing says Walt Disney World® Resort more than Mickey Mouse and the monorail, so what better way to start your day than a buffet breakfast with Mickey Mouse, Minnie Mouse, Pluto, Donald Duck and Goofy under the roar of the monorail. Head to **Chef Mickey's** (📞407-939-3463; 4600 World Dr, Disney's Contemporary Resort; adult/child from $41/25; ⏱7-11:15am, 11:30am-2:30pm &

5-9:30pm) for an early breakfast (reservations are required well in advance).

❷ Fantasyland Rides

While it's tempting to meander down Main Street, admiring the windows and picking up souvenirs, lines at Disney old-school classics soon stretch beyond an hour so you'll want to get to them first thing. Head to Fantasyland, just beyond the castle, and ride **Peter Pan's Flight**, **Many Adventures of Winnie-the-Pooh** and **Mad Tea Party**, in that order.

❸ Space Mountain

Scurry over to Tomorrowland for SpaceMountain, an outer-space-themed indoor roller coaster that first opened in 1975. The premise here is that you are riding a spaceship through the stratosphere, and the entire ride takes place in darkness with only twinkling stars and zooming galaxies as light.

❹ Disney Animatronic Classics

Some of Magic Kingdom's earliest attractions feel strikingly bizarre and kitsch by today's standards, and that's their charm. Take a slow-moving ride past animatronic elephants on the **Jungle Cruise**, pop into **Walt Disney's Enchanted Tiki Room** to watch animatronic birds sing, and ride around the world past singing-and-dancing animatronic children in **It's a Small World**.

❺ Splash Mountain

Hop on a boat and ride through the 1946 film *Song of the South*, past animatronic Brer Fox and Brer Bear, around through the darkness and up, up, up...until you splash down into the water.

❻ Dine with a Princess

If you've little ones, reserve ahead to dine with a princess at **Cinderella's Royal Table** (☏ 407-934-2927; Cinderella's Castle; adult/child from $60/35; ⊗8-10:15am, 11:30am-2:50pm & 4-10:20pm (hours vary); ☏), or go the whole **Bibbidi Bobbidi Boo** (☏ 407-939-7895; hair & makeup from $60; ⊗10am-8pm, hours vary) transformation where a fairy godmother finalizes your kid's transformation from shorts and T-shirt to bedazzling princess with fanciful hairstyling and makeup.

❼ Parades & Concerts

Magic Kingdom offers parades and concerts (on the steps of Cinderella's Castle) throughout the day. Check the schedule as you come in. You can't reserve a place until the cordons go up, so don't panic about not getting a curb-front seat. The floats are high enough that you'll see something even if you're not in the front row. Return to the park in the evening for the Nighttime Spectacular (called **Happily Ever After** at the time of writing; though the names do change).

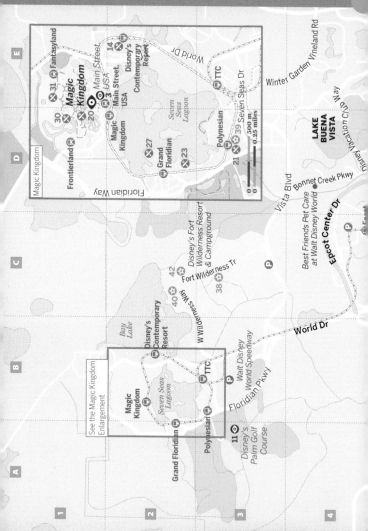

Downtown Disney

See Downtown Disney Enlargement

Downtown Disney

Falcon's Fire Golf Club

S International Dr

W Osceola Pkwy

Central Florida Greenway (toll)

Village Amphicar Lake

Characters in Flight

Tours **15**

12

44

45

35 **43**

22

9

37 **41**

4

DisneyQuest Indoor Interactive Theme Park E Buena Vista Dr

36

Downtown Disney

0   400 m
0   0.2 miles

Typhoon 1 Lagoon

E Buena Vista Dr

32

24 **5**

29

Frozen Ever After

28 **26** **16**

6 **33**

Epcot Resort

Disney's BoardWalk

Fantasia Gardens and Fairways Miniature Golf **10**

2 Blizzard Beach

W Buena Vista Dr

Disney's Hollywood Studios

25

Osceola Pkwy

ESPN Wide World of Sports

Irlo Bronson Memorial Hwy

World Dr

World Dr

Rafiki's Planet 7 Watch

Discovery Island

34 Oasis

8

13

Disney's Animal Kingdom

Osceola Pkwy

Sherbeth Rd

19

18

17

For reviews see	
⊙ Top Sights	p24
⊙ Sights	p46
⊗ Eating	p48
⊓ Drinking	p53
⊕ Entertainment	p54
⊓ Shopping	p57

0   2 km
0   1 miles

Sights

Typhoon Lagoon
AMUSEMENT PARK

1 Map p44, D5

An abundance of palm trees, a zero-entry pool with a white sandy beach, high-speed slides and the best wave pool in Orlando make this one of the most beautiful water parks in Florida. Little ones will love floating along **Castaway Creek** and splashing at **Ketchakiddee Creek**. (☑407-939-5277, 407-560-4120; www.disneyworld.disney. go.com; 1145 Buena Vista Dr, Walt Disney World®; adult/child $53/45, prices vary daily; ⏱hours vary; ⬛Disney)

Blizzard Beach
AMUSEMENT PARK

2 Map p44, B6

The newer of Disney's two water parks, themed as a melted Swiss ski resort complete with a ski lift, Blizzard Beach is the 1980s Vegas Strip hotel to Typhoon Lagoon's Bellagio. At its center sits **Mt Gushmore**, from which water slides burst forth. (☑407-939-5277, 407-560-3400; www.disney. disney.go.com; 1534 Blizzard Beach Dr, Walt Disney World®; adult/child $53/45, incl in Water Park Fun & More with Magic Your Way theme park ticket; ⏱hours vary; ⬛Disney)

Main Street, USA
AREA

3 Map p44, E1

Fashioned after Walt Disney's hometown of Marceline, MO, Main Street, USA, is best experienced with an aimless meander. Peruse the miniature dioramas of Peter Pan and Snow White

in the street windows; pop in to catch the black-and-white movie reels of old Disney cartoons, and browse the hundreds of thousands of must-have Disney souvenirs. (www.disneyworld.disney. go.com; Magic Kingdom; theme-park admission required; ⏱9am-9pm, hours vary; ⬛; ⬛Disney, ⬛Disney, ⬛Lynx 50, 56)

DisneyQuest Indoor Interactive Theme Park
AMUSEMENT PARK

4 Map p44, D8

With five dizzying floors of exhibits designed to indulge video-game addicts, this 'interactive theme park' makes the perfect place to while away a rainy or hot afternoon. Virtual-reality attractions include a trip on Aladdin's magic carpet over Agrabah and a float down a river into the Mesozoic Age. You can design and 'ride' your own roller coaster, or simply lose yourself for hours in old-school video games and pinball machines. (☑407-828-3800; www.disneyworld.disney.go.com; 1620 East Buena Vista Dr, Disney Springs; ⏱noon-9pm; ⬛; ⬛Disney, ⬛Disney, ⬛Lynx 50)

Frozen Ever After
RIDE

5 Map p44, C5

One of Disney's current 'hot' rides, Frozen Ever After takes you on an ancient Norwegian vessel as you sail off into the wintery world of *Frozen*, set to your favorite *Frozen* tunes, of course. *Frozen* friends make appearances and there's plenty of special effects. Not too much detail: we don't

Blizzard Beach

want to thaw your expectations here. (https://disneyworld.disney.go.com/attractions/epcot/frozen-ever-after/; Norway, Epcot; ⊙9am-6pm, hours vary)

Disney's BoardWalk   WATERFRONT

6 ⊙ Map p44, C5

Far less harried and crowded than Disney Springs, the very small Disney's BoardWalk area across from Epcot and along Crescent Lake echoes waterfront boardwalks of turn-of-the-century New England seaside resorts. On Thursday to Saturday evenings magicians, jugglers and musicians give a festive vibe, and there are a handful of good restaurants and bars. Pick up a doughnut or cute lil' Mickey Mouse cakes at the bakery, and toot around on a surrey-with-the-fringe-on-top bike. (☎407-939-5277; www.disneyworld.disney.go.com; 2101 Epcot Resorts Blvd, Walt Disney World®; ⬛Disney, ⬤Disney)

Rafiki's Planet Watch   ZOO

7 ⊙ Map p44, A5

Veterinarians care for sick and injured animals at the **Conservation Station**. You can check out pet sheep and goats at **Affection Section**. On the **Habitat Habit!** trail check out the adorable, fist-sized tamarin monkeys. But ultimately, the **Wildlife Express Train** you take to get here might just be the best part of this Disney enigma. (www.disneyworld.disney.go.com; Animal Kingdom; theme-park admission required; ⊙9am-6pm, hours vary; 👶; ⬛Disney)

Discovery Island
AREA

8 ◉ Map p44, A6

The only attraction here is the *Bugs' Life*–themed **It's Tough to Be a Bug!**, a 4D movie that includes periods of darkness, dry ice and flashing lights. Though it's a lot of fun and very cute, it can terrify little ones – you will definitely hear children crying by the end. (www.disneyworld.disney.go.com; Animal Kingdom; theme-park admission required; ⊙9am-6pm, hours vary; ☐Disney)

Characters in Flight
RIDE

9 ◉ Map p44, E8

Guests climb onboard the basket of this massive tethered gas balloon and ascend 400ft into the air for 360-degree views. Between 8:30am and 10am they offer a special for $10 per person. (☏407-939-7529; www.disneyworld. disney.go.com; 1620 East Buena Vista Dr, Disney Springs; adult/child $18/15; ⊙8:30am-midnight; ☐Disney, ⚓Disney, ☐Lynx 50)

Fantasia Gardens and Fairways Miniature Golf
GOLF

10 ◉ Map p44, C5

Two fairyland-themed courses based on the classic animation *Fantasia*. (☏407-560-4870; www.disneyworld.disney. go.com; 1205 Epcot Resorts Blvd, Walt Disney World®; adult/child $14/12; ⊙10am-11pm)

Disney's Palm Golf Course
GOLF

11 ◉ Map p44, A3

This Arnold Palmer–designed, 18-hole championship course is one of Disney's most picturesque, with palm trees, lakes and sloping greens. (☏407-939-4653; www.golfwdw.com; 1950 W Magnolia Palm Dr, Disney's Grand Floridian Resort & Spa; per round from $40)

Amphicar Tours
BOATING

12 ◉ Map p44, E8

Go for a spin in these extraordinary, genuine German vintage amphicars. They drive on land and then enter the water for a tour of waterside Disney Springs. Pricey, but definitely a once-in-a-lifetime experience. The mooring is next to the Boathouse. (☏407-939-2628; www.theboathouseorlando.com; 1620 East Buena Vista Dr, Disney Springs; up to 3 people 25min $125; ⊙10am-10pm; ☐Disney, ⚓Disney, ☐Lynx 50)

Oasis
ZOO

13 ◉ Map p44, A6

Oasis is the first themed section of Animal Kingdom. It has cool critters, including a giant anteater, but it's best to move along to other attractions and pause to enjoy the animals on your way out. (www.disneyworld.disney.go.com; Animal Kingdom; theme-park admission required; ⊙9am-6pm, hours vary; 🚹; ☐Disney)

Eating

California Grill
AMERICAN $$$

14 ✕ Map p44, E2

Earning consistent oohs and aahs from locals and repeat Disney guests, this rooftop classic boasts magnificent views of Magic Kingdom fireworks and offers everything from quirky sushi to triple-cheese flatbread. Reservations are very difficult to secure, so make them as close to 180 days in advance as possible. (📞407-939-3463; www. disneyworld.disney.go.com; 4600 World Dr, Disney's Contemporary Resort; mains $36-51; ⏱5-10pm; 🚲; 🚌Disney, 🚢Disney, 🚝Disney)

Paddlefish

INTERNATIONAL **$$$**

15 🍴   Map p44, E8

This paddle steamer has had an entire revamp and reopened in February 2016. It's smart, contemporary and chic. Its lovely dining areas are ingeniously incorporated into different parts of the boat, so you have a choice of ambience: over water, at the stern or snuggled in elsewhere. It's the place to go for a leisurely and sophisticated meal. (www.disneyworld.disney.go.com; 1620 East Buena Vista Dr, Disney Springs; mains $25-40; ⏱11:30am-11pm; 🚌Disney, 🚢Disney, 🚌Lynx 50)

Tutto Gusto

ITALIAN **$$**

16 🍴   Map p44, C5

Full marks for this authentic Italian brasserie and wine bar. It oozes style and serves up excellent small plates, including meats and cheeses. Definitely the place to come for an excellent glass of Italian wine and homemade pasta served at the bar, high bar tables or while you are nestled cozily in a sofa. Recommended for dinner before the night spectaculars at Epcot. (📞407-939-3463; https:// disneyworld.disney.go.com/dining/epcot/

tutto-gusto-wine-cellar/; Italy, Epcot; mains $12-18; ⏱11:30am-9pm; ❄🛜)

Boma

BUFFET **$$$**

17 🍴   Map p44, A6

Several steps above Disney's usual buffet options, this African-inspired eatery offers wood-roasted meats, interesting soups such as coconut curried chicken and plenty of salads. Handsomely furnished with dark woods, decorated with African art and tapestries, and flanked by garden-view windows on one side, Boma offers not only good food but unusually calm and pleasant surrounds. (📞407-939-3463, 407-938-4744; www.disneyworld. disney.go.com; 2901 Osceola Pkwy, Disney's Animal Kingdom Lodge; adult/child breakfast $24.50/13, dinner $40.50/21; ⏱7:30-11am & 5-9:30pm; 🛜🚲; 🚌Disney)

Sanaa

AFRICAN **$$**

18 🍴   Map p44, A6

Lovely cafe with Savannah views – giraffes, ostriches and zebras graze

Top Tip

On Your Bike

More than a dozen bike-rental places throughout Walt Disney World® rent on a first-come, first-served basis. A few places, including Disney's BoardWalk, rent out two-, four- and six-person surrey bikes, with four wheels, candy-striped tops and bench seats.

outside the window. You almost forget you're in Florida, but, hey, that's Disney. Try slow-cooked and tandoori chicken, ribs, lamb or shrimp; the delicious salad sampler with tasty watermelon, cucumber and fennel salad; and a mango margarita. (📞407-939-3463; www.disneyworld.disney.go.com; 3701 Osceola Pkwy, Kidani Village, Disney's Animal Kingdom Lodge; mains $17-26; ⏱11:30am-3pm & 5-9:30pm; 🍴👶; 🚌Disney)

Jiko - The Cooking Place
AFRICAN $$$

19 🍴 Map p44, A6

Excellent food, with plenty of grains, vegetables and creative twists, a tiny bar and rich African surrounds make this a Disney favorite for both quality and theming. You can relax with a glass of wine on the hotel's back deck, alongside the giraffes and other African beasts. For a less-expensive option, enjoy an appetizer (the Taste of Africa features various dips and crackers) at the bar. (📞407-938-4733, 407-939-3463; www.disneyworld.disney. go.com; 2901 Osceola Pkwy, Disney's Animal Kingdom Lodge; mains $41-55; ⏱5:30-10pm; 🍴👶; 🚌Disney)

Jungle Navigation Co. Ltd Skipper Canteen
INTERNATIONAL $$

20 🍴 Map p44, D1

This adventure-themed spot harks back to days of boat exploration. It has three delightful areas based around boat skippers' tropical headquarters. Enjoy a meal in the Secret Society of Adventurer's Room, the Jungle Room

or the Mess. It's the most atmospheric of options in the park and the meals are large, but by far the healthiest. (www.disneyworld.disney.go.com; Magic Kingdom; mains $17-30; ⏱11:30am-9pm)

'Ohana
POLYNESIAN $$

21 🍴 Map p44, D3

The Polynesian's signature restaurant evokes a South Pacific feel with rock-art animals, a huge oak-burning grill cooking up massive kebabs of meat, and demonstrations of hula and limbo dancing, coconut racing and other Polynesian-themed shenanigans. The only thing on the menu is the all-you-can-eat family-style kebabs and veggies, slid off skewers directly onto the giant wok-like platters on the table. (📞407-939-3463; www.disneyworld. disney.go.com; 1600 Seven Seas Dr, Disney's Polynesian Resort; feast $35-39; ⏱7:30am-noon & 3:30-10pm; 👶; 🚌Disney, 🚢Disney)

Frontera Cocina
MEXICAN $$

22 🍴 Map p44, E8

A smart, trendy version of modern Mexico where, thanks to Chef Rick Bayless, corn, chili and salsa are whipped up into contemporary tastes in a delightfully light, bright and bustling environment. A pleasant change from some southern flavors. Fun margarita-filled happy hours, too. (📞407-560-9197; www.fronteracocina.com; 1620 East Buena Vista Dr, Disney Springs; mains $22-34; ⏱11am-10pm Sun-Wed, 11am-10.45pm Thu-Mon, 🚌Disney, 🚢Disney, 🚌Lynx 50)

Victoria & Albert's
AMERICAN $$$

23 Map p44, D2

Indulge yourself in the earthy, cream-colored, Victorian-inspired decor at this elegant restaurant, the crème de la crème of Orlando's dining scene and one of its most coveted reservations. The meal, complete with crystal and live cello music, oozes romance. You must reserve directly (not through Disney World's Dining number). Dinner at the intimate Chef's Table or Queen Victoria's room includes 13 courses. Children must be aged 10 and over. (☏407-939-3862; www.victoria-alberts.com; 4401 Floridian Way, Disney's Grand Floridian Resort; prix-fixe from $185, wine pairing from $65; ⏰5-9:20pm; 🎧; 🚌Disney, 🚤Disney, 🚝Disney)

La Cantina de San Angel
MEXICAN $

24 Map p44, C5

One of the best fast-food places in the park. Try the tacos, served with surprisingly tasty *pico de gallo* (fresh salsa of tomatoes, onion and jalapeños) and fresh avocado. Great guacamole, too. (www.disneyworld.disney.go.com; Mexico, Epcot; mains $11-13, theme park admission required; ⏰11am-park closing; 🎧🖊; 🚌Disney, 🚤Disney)

Hollywood Brown Derby Lounge
TAPAS $$

25 Map p44, C6

Upscale, small-bite menu with lump-crab cocktail, mussels and beef sliders, and an excellent selection of cocktails. It's generally pretty easy to snag a table at the bistro-style sidewalk patio, a great place to relax and people-watch over a flight of scotch, champagne, martinis or margaritas, or order a drink to go. Not exactly fast food, but reservations are not accepted. (📞407-939-3463; www.disneyworld.disney.go.com; Hollywood Studios; tapas $8-18; ⏱11am-park closing; 🛜🚻; 🚆Disney, 🚢Disney)

Les Halles Boulangerie Patisserie
FRENCH $

26 🍴 Map p44, C5

Most folks come for cakes, éclairs and cookies, but it also sells French-bread pizza, quiche and those baguette sandwiches that are ubiquitous in France, as well as wine and champagne. (www.disneyworld.disney.go.com; France, Epcot; snacks $5-12, theme-park admission required; ⏱9am-park closing; 🚆Disney, 🚢Disney)

Narcoossee's
SEAFOOD $$$

27 🍴 Map p44, D2

Muted waterfront dining on the boat dock at the Grand Floridian makes a convenient, relaxing and lovely respite if you've been at Magic Kingdom for the afternoon and want to return after dinner for the fireworks. Though offering primarily seafood, it also serves duck, filet mignon and ahi tuna.

The porch is a good place from which to watch the fireworks in any case. (📞407-939-3463; www.disneyworld.disney.go.com; 4401 Floridian Way, Disney's Grand Floridian Resort; mains $39-67; ⏱5-9:30pm; 🚻; 🚆Disney, 🚢Disney, 🚤Disney)

Flying Fish
SEAFOOD $$$

28 🍴 Map p44, C5

Sspecializing in complicated and innovative seafood dishes, this consistently ranks as one of the best upscale dining spots at Disney. It's a contemporary, slick spot with a modern ocean theme. Be sure to reserve ahead. Kids' meals are significantly cheaper (from $13 to $17). (📞407-939-2359, 407-939-3463; www.disneyworld.disney.go.com; Disney's BoardWalk; mains $37-59; ⏱5-9:30pm; 🚲🚻; 🚢Disney)

Akershus Royal Banquet Hall
NORWEGIAN $$$

29 🍴 Map p44, C5

Join Disney princesses (a selection of Snow White, Cinderella, Belle, Aurora or Ariel) for a Norwegian-inspired feast in medieval surrounds – Disney-style, of course, so you'll find pizza and lemonade with a glowing Ariel alongside Norwegian meatballs with lingonberries. One of the better character meals, both in terms of ambience and food. (📞407-939-3463; www.disneyworld.disney.go.com; Norway, Epcot; buffet $35-60, theme-park admission required; ⏱8-11am, noon-3:30pm & 5-8:30pm; 🚢Disney, 🚆Disney)

Columbia Harbour House
AMERICAN $

30 🍴 Map p44, D1

Decent vegetarian chili, unusually tasty clam chowder, chicken potpie and salmon. The interior is charming as you're inside an old boat that has 'docked' in the US, having come from the UK. (Use your imagination: this

is Walt Disney World® after all). (www.
disneyworld.disney.go.com; Magic Kingdom;
mains $10-15, theme-park admission required;
🕐11am-park closing; 🛜👶; 🚌Disney,
🚢Disney, 🚌Lynx 50, 56)

Gaston's Tavern AMERICAN $

31 🍴 Map p44, E1

Homage to that superego Gaston,
with giant cinnamon rolls and hummus. It's an odd mix of quick-service
options, but the re-created tavern
with the giant portrait of Gaston is
well done. Try Le Fou's Brew, Disney's
counter to Universal's runaway hit
Butterbeer. (www.disneyworld.disney.
go.com; Magic Kingdom; mains $6-16, theme-
park admission required; 🕐9am-park closing;
🛜👶; 🚌Disney, 🚢Disney, 🚌Lynx 50, 56)

Drinking

La Cava del Tequila BAR

32 🍸 Map p44, D5

Pop in for a cucumber, passion fruit or
blood-orange margarita. Can't decide?
Try a flight of margaritas or shots. The
menu features more than 220 types of
tequila, and it's a cozy, dark spot, with
tiled floors, Mexican-styled murals and
a beamed ceiling. (☎407-939-3463; www.
disneyworld.disney.go.com; Mexico, Epcot;
theme-park admission required; 🕐11am-park
closing; 🚌Disney, 🚢Disney, 🚌Disney)

Jock Lindsay's BAR

According to, er...'old' Disney folklore,
Jock (the pilot in *Raiders of the Lost
Ark*) 'arrived here in 1938 while chas-

ing down a mythology-based tip in
central Florida.' He liked the natural
springs and lush terrain, and so bought
some land. His hangar, his home base'
(see 12 ◉ Map p44, E8), became popular
for world travelers and locals...and
here you now are. (www.disneyworld.disney.
go.com; 1620 East Buena Vista Dr, Disney
Springs; 🕐11:30am-midnight; 🚌Disney,
🚢Disney, 🚌Lynx 50)

Belle Vue Room BAR

33 🍸 Map p44, C5

On the 2nd floor of Disney's Board-
Walk Inn, this is an excellent place for
a quiet drink. It's more like a sitting
room: you can relax and play a board
game, listen to classic radio shows
such as *Lone Ranger,* or simply take
your drink to a rocking chair on the
balcony and watch the comings and
goings along Disney's Boardwalk.
(☎407-939-6200; www.disneyworld.disney.
go.com; 2101 Epcot Resorts Blvd, Disney's
BoardWalk Inn; 🕐6:30-11am & 5pm-midnight;
🚌Disney, 🚢Disney)

Boathouse BAR

A series of three bars are spread over
this smart waterfront place (see 12 ◉
Map p44, E8), with classic craft cocktails
and a good wine list (that showcases
American wines). Nightly music enter-
tains you well into the morning. After
a drink or three, head off for a spin
and a float in a genuine amphicar
(p48). (☎407-939-2628; www.theboathouse
orlando.com; 1620 East Buena Vista Dr, Disney
Springs; 🕐11am-1:30am)

Dawa Bar
BAR

34 Map p44, A5

The best place in Animal Kingdom for a cocktail. Sidle up to the flat-roofed bar, kind of like an African 'shebeen', and order a sugarcane mojito and rest those Disney-weary bones. (www.disneyworld.disney.go.com; Animal Kingdom; theme-park admission required; 11am-park closing; Disney)

Big River Grille & Brewing Works
BREWERY

Open-air microbrewery (see 6 Map p44, C5) with unique brews sold only on location, plus soups and pastas. Lovely outdoor seating along the water. (407-560-0253; www.disneyworld.disney.go.com; Disney's BoardWalk; 11am-11pm)

Local Life
Screenings & Performances

Go to www.buildabettermousetrip.com/activity-outdoormovie.php for a schedule of free outdoor screenings of Disney movies at Disney hotels and other locales at Disney's Fort Wilderness.

You'll find fabulous performances in each of the parks. In Disney Springs, Cirque du Soleil La Nouba fuses gymnastic superfeats with dance, light, music...and Disney.

Tambu Lounge
BAR

Escape to the islands (see 39 Map p44, D3), Disney-style, with umbrella-topped tropical drinks and Blue Glow-tinis. There's also an excellent selection of bar food, including pulled pork nachos and kebabs, and it's an easy boat or monorail from here to Magic Kingdom. (www.disneyworld.disney.go.com; Disney's Polynesian Resort; Disney, Disney)

Raglan Road
PUB

35 Map p44, E8

Traditional Irish ditties. Irish dancing, solid tasty fare, cozy pub decor and beer flights with Guinness, Harp, Smithwicks and Kilkenny complete the leprechaun mood. (407-938-0300; www.raglanroad.com; 1620 East Buena Vista Dr, Disney Springs; 10am-2am; Disney, Disney)

ESPN Club
SPORTS BAR

So many TVs screening here (see 28 Map p44, C5) the hottest games that even in the bathroom you won't miss a single play. (407-939-5100; www.disneyworld.disney.go.com; Disney's BoardWalk; 11am-midnight)

Entertainment

Disney Springs
AREA

36 Map p44, E8

The primary entertainment district in Walt Disney World® – with shops, restaurants and bars, live music and a movie theater – stretches along the

JOHN GREIM/AGE FOTOSTOCKS ©

waterfront. You can take buses from Disney resorts to Disney Springs, and a few hotels offer boat transport to the area, but you cannot take Disney transport from here to any theme or water parks. Admission and parking is free. (☑407-939-6244; www.disneyworld.disney.go.com; 1490 E Buena Vista Dr, Walt Disney World®; ⊙8:30am-2am; ☒Disney, ☒Disney, ☒Lynx 50)

Cirque du Soleil La Nouba
PERFORMING ARTS

37 ⭐ Map p44, D8

Disney's best live show features mind-boggling acrobatic feats expertly fused to light, stage and costume design to create a cohesive artistic vision. And of course, there's a silly Disney twist

involving a princess and a frog. This is a small horseshoe theater, with roughly 20 rows from the stage to the top, and no balcony. (☑407-939-7328, 407-939-7600; www.cirquedusoleil.com; 1478 Buena Vista Dr, Disney Springs; adult $59-139, child $48-115; ⊙6pm & 9pm Tue-Sat; ☒Disney, ☒Disney, ☒Lynx 50)

Chip 'n' Dale Campfire Singalong
CINEMA

38 ⭐ Map p44, C3

This intimate and low-key character experience offers singing and dancing with Chip and Dale, campfires for roasting marshmallows, and a free outdoor screening of a Disney film. Every night is a different movie, and Disney doesn't post a schedule on its website – call or search online. (☎407-939-7529; www.disneyworld.disney. go.com; 4510 N Wilderness Trail, Disney's Fort Wilderness Resort; ⏰7pm winter, 8pm summer; 🚌Disney, ⛴Disney)

Spirit of Aloha DANCE

39 ⭐ Map p44, D3

Hula-clad men and women leap around the stage, dance and play with fire in this South Pacific–style luau at Disney's Polynesian Resort. Pulled pork, barbecue ribs and island-themed specialties like pineapple-coconut bread are served family-style. (☎407-939-3463; www.disneyworld.disney.go.com; 1600 Seven Seas Dr, Disney's Polynesian Resort; adult $66-78, child 3-9yr $39-46; ⏰5:15pm & 8:15pm; 🚌Disney, ⛴Disney, 🚝Disney)

Hoop-Dee-Doo Musical Revue COMEDY

40 ⭐ Map p44, C2

Nineteenth-century vaudeville show at Disney's Fort Wilderness Resort, with

ribs delivered to your table in metal buckets, corny jokes and the audience singing along to 'Hokey Pokey' and 'My Darling Clementine.' This is one of Disney's longest-running shows and is great fun, once you grab your washboard and get into the spirit of it all. (☎407-939-3463; www.disneyworld.disney. go.com; 4510 N Wilderness Trail, Disney's Fort Wilderness Resort; adult $64-72, child 3-9yr $38-43; ⏰4pm, 6:15pm & 8:30pm daily; ♿; 🚌Disney, ⛴Disney)

House of Blues LIVE MUSIC

41 ⭐ Map p44, D8

Top acts visit this national chain serving Southern cooking and blues. It's particularly popular for the Sunday Gospel Brunch buffet. (☎407-934-2583; www.houseofblues.com; 1490 Buena Vista Dr, Disney Springs; ⏰10am-11pm Mon-Thu, to midnight Fri & Sat, 10:30am-11pm Sun; 📶♿; 🚌Disney, ⛴Disney, 🚌Lynx 50)

Mickey's Backyard Barbecue COMEDY

42 ⭐ Map p44, C2

The only dinner theater with Disney characters. Join in on country-and-western singin', ho-down style-stompin' and goofy Mickey antics at this Disney favorite. (☎407-939-3463; www.disneyworld.disney.go.com; 4510 N Fort Wilderness Trail, Disney's Fort Wilderness Resort; adult $62-72, child 3-9yr $37-47; ⏰hours vary; ♿; 🚌Disney, ⛴Disney)

Top Tip

Shop Around the World

For an international twist to your Disney souvenir, walk around the world at Epcot. Buy a belly-dancer kit in Morocco, tartan shawls and Mickey Mouse shortbread cookies in the UK, and so on. It's commercial, but it's amazing how much people will open their purse when on holiday (beware!).

HELEN SESSIONS / ALAMY STOCK PHOTO ©

Disney's Hollywood Studios (p38)

Shopping

Lego Imagination Center   TOYS

43 🔒 Map p44, E8

Life-size Lego creations, tables to create your own masterpieces and a wall of individually priced Lego pieces. (☏407-828-0065; www.disneyworld. disney.go.com; 1672 Buena Vista Dr, Disney Springs; ⏰9am-11pm; 🚊Disney, 🚢Disney, 🚌Lynx 50)

Once Upon a Toy   TOYS

44 🔒 Map p44, E8

Design a personalized My Little Pony, build your own light saber and create your own tiara at one of the best toy stores anywhere. You'll find old-school classics such as Mr Potato Head and Lincoln Logs, board games, action figures, stuffed animals and more. (☏407-824-4321; www.disneyworld.disney. go.com; 1375 Buena Vista Dr, Disney Springs; ⏰10am-11:30pm; 🚊Disney, 🚢Disney, 🚌Lynx 50)

World of Disney   GIFTS & SOUVENIRS

45 🔒 Map p44, E8

Room after room of Disney everything at this Disney mega-super-duper store (the country's largest). (☏407-939-6224; www.disneyworld.disney.go.com; Disney Springs; ⏰9am-11pm; 🚊Disney, 🚢Disney, 🚌Lynx 50)

Explore

Universal Orlando Resort

Pedestrian-friendly Universal Orlando Resort has got spunk, spirit and attitude. With fantastic rides, excellent children's attractions and entertaining shows, it's comparable to Walt Disney World®. But Universal does everything just a bit smarter, funnier and more smoothly, as well as being smaller and easier to navigate. Universal offers unabashed, adrenaline-pumped, full-speed-ahead fun for the entire family.

The Sights in a Day

☀️ Beat the crowds with an early start at **Wizarding World of Harry Potter – Diagon Alley** (p61). Ride Escape from Gringotts, stop at Ollivanders Shop, eat breakfast at the **Leaky Cauldron** (p71) and take in the sights before hopping on the Hogwarts Express to **Hogsmeade** (p65).

☀️ Ride Harry Potter and the Forbidden Journey and Dragon Challenge, poke through the cobbled streets and grab a Butterbeer to sip on your way to lunch at **Confisco Grille** (p72). Afterwards, ride the water plumes, coasters and simulated delights at **Islands of Adventure** (p64), then catch the Hogwarts Express back to London for top sights at **Universal Studios** (p60). Finish the day with a waterfront mojito at **Chez Alcatraz** (p75).

🌙 Good wine, old-fashioned soda in a bottle, and a bowl of pasta at **Mama Della's Ristorante** (p71) make a relaxing end to the sensory overload of the park, for both kids and adults.

👁️ Top Sights

Universal Studios (p60)

Islands of Adventure (p64)

💜 Best of Universal Orlando Resort

Dining
Mama Della's Ristorante (p71)

Emeril's Tchoup Chop (p72)

Drinking & Nightlife
Strong Water Tavern (p75)

Velvet Bar (p75)

Entertainment
Blue Man Group (p77)

Getting There

🚗 **Car** I-4 east-bound exit 75A, west-bound exit 74B.

🚌 **Shuttle** Area hotels offer scheduled shuttle service to Universal Orlando Resort.

🚋 **I-Trolley** Circulates I-Drive.

🚌 **Bus** Lynx 21, 37 and 40.

◉ Top Sights
Universal Studios

Universal Studios' simulation-heavy rides and shows are dedicated to silver-screen and TV icons. Ride through a theme park with Bart Simpson, walk through Muggles London to Diagon Alley, and sidle up to Lucille Ball on Hollywood Blvd. Universal Studios, themed as a Hollywood backlot, is geographically divided by region-specific architecture and ambience.

👁 Map p68, C2

📞 407-363-8000

www.universalorlando.com

1000 Universal Studios Plaza, Universal Orlando Resort

adult 1/2 days $105/185, child $100/175

⏱from 9am (closing hours vary)

Wizarding World of Harry Potter – Diagon Alley

Wizarding World of Harry Potter – Diagon Alley

Diagon Alley, lined with magical shops selling robes, Quidditch supplies, wands, scaly creatures and more, leads to the massive Gringotts Bank. Detour through the blackness of Knockturn Alley, where only dark wizards go to buy their supplies, hydrate with an elixir of Fire Protection Potion poured into Gilly Water, try a scoop of Butterbeer ice cream and, when you hear the grumblings of the bank's ferocious dragon, perched on the top, be prepared for his fiery roar.

Springfield

In 2013 Universal opened Simpsons-themed **Springfield**, home to that iconic American TV family. Hang at **Moe's Tavern** (drinks $3-9; ⊙11am-park closing; 🤚), grab doughnuts at Lard Lad, and meet Krusty the Clown, Sideshow Bob and the Simpson family themselves. The child-friendly Kang & Kodos' Twirl & Hurl offers an interactive twist to whirling and don't miss **The Simpsons Ride** (Express Pass), a simulated extravaganza into Krusty the Clown's techno-colored theme park, Krustyland.

E.T. Adventure

This is one of Universal's classic rides and one for the nostalgia seekers. For some people, *E.T.* is Universal. Jump aboard the flying bicycle and assist E.T. to save the planet. Dodge the baddies while soaring into the stars and into E.T.'s magical world. Sure it might be dated compared to some hi-tech 'competitors,' but it's sweet. And after all, who can resist a little, shriveled alien.

☑ Top Tips

▶ Many attractions are in the form of shows; check your park map for showtimes upon arrival and plan accordingly.

▶ Free wi-fi is available throughout the park and Universal's free app features live wait times.

▶ Hit the Wizarding World of Harry Potter – Diagon Alley's Escape from Gringotts ride when the park gates open, as lines can be hours long and it doesn't offer Express Pass access. Guests of Universal Orlando Resort hotels can enter one hour early.

✕ Take a Break

Head to Central Park, a grassy area with shade trees, flowers and lagoon views.

New York

Revenge of the Mummy (Express Pass) combines roller-coaster speed and twists with in-your-face special effects. Head deep into ancient Egyptian catacombs in near pitch black, but don't anger Imhotep the mummy – in his wrath he flings you past fire, water and more.

Production Central

Home to two of Universal's most talked-about rides, the incredible 3D simulation **Transformers: The Ride 3-D** (Express Pass), which is even fun for folks who don't know anything about them; and the high-thrill coaster **Hollywood Rip Ride Rockit** (Express Pass). This massive roller coaster is not for the faint of heart – you Rip up to 65mph, Ride 17 stories above the theme park, around a loop-dee-loop, and down a crazy-steep drop, and Rockit to customized music.

Despicable Me: Minion Mayhem

Fans of *Despicable Me* won't want to miss the chance to become one of Gru's minions in this 3D **simulation** (⏱from 9am). There's lots of goofy fun in the best of minion traditions, and there's nothing particularly scary. Even Express Pass+ lines here can soar upwards from 30 minutes, so come first thing.

World Expo

The main attraction here is **Men in Black Alien Attack** (Express Pass), a 3D interactive video game that is a lot of fun but not at all scary. Swing and spin through a danger-laden downtown Manhattan, with all kinds of silly looking aliens around the place, peeking out of windows and snuffling through the garage. This is a slow-moving ride and as you cruise along you must aim and shoot your lasers (at the so-called 'scum of the universe' – yikes) to rack up points.

London

To enter the Wizarding World of Harry Potter, you must, of course, start in London. Like the rest of Universal Studios, it's themed with great detail to create a sense of place – and it isn't just any London, it's the London of JK Rowling's imagination, the London shared by wizards and muggles alike. Check out the purple, triple-decker Knight Bus (don't miss peering into the inside from the back) and look out for Kreacher the House Elf peeking from behind the curtain in the Grimmauld Place brownstones. There are no traditional rides, but you catch the Hogwarts Express from King's Cross Station here.

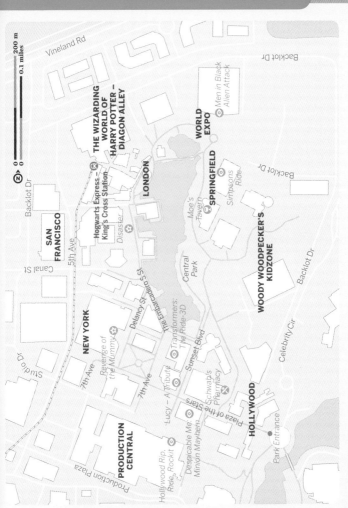

Top Sights
Islands of Adventure

One of Universal Orlando Resort's four theme parks, Islands of Adventure delivers over-the-top, evocative theming and oodles of honest-to-goodness fun. Expect everything from your favorite superhero to roller coasters, memories from childhood picture books and animations, plus those rides that get you wet, wet, wet! The park is divided into distinct areas: cartoon-heavy Toon Island, the dinosaur-themed Jurassic Park and more, each with rides, play areas and dining.

👁 Map p68, B3

📞 407-363-8000

www.universalorlando.com

6000 Universal Blvd, Universal Orlando Resort

adult 1/2 days $105/185, child $100/175

🕐 from 9am (closing hours vary)

Jurassic Park River Adventure

Wizarding World of Harry Potter – Hogsmeade

Poke along the cobbled streets and impossibly crooked buildings of **Hogsmeade** (☉9am-6pm, hours vary), sip frothy Butterbeer, munch on Cauldron Cakes and mail a card via Owl Post, all in the shadow of Hogwarts Castle. The detail and authenticity tickle the fancy at every turn, from the screeches of the mandrakes in the shop windows to the groans of Moaning Myrtle in the bathroom – keep your eyes peeled for magical happenings.

Jurassic Park River Adventure

Jurassic Park (☉9am-6pm, hours vary) floats you gently past friendly vegetarian dinosaurs, and all seems well and good until...things go wrong and those grass-munchin' cuties are replaced with the stuff of nightmares. To escape the looming teeth of the giant T-rex, you plunge 85ft to the water below. Young children might be terrified by the creatures, the dark and the plunge.

Marvel Super Hero Island

Bright, loud and fast moving, **Marvel Super Hero Island** (☉9am-6pm, hours vary) is sensory overload and a thrill-lover's paradise. Don't miss the motion simulator **Amazing Adventures of Spider-Man** (Express Pass recommended), where super villains rendered in incredible 3D are on the loose, jumping on your car and chasing you around the streets of New York City, and the wild and crazy **Incredible Hulk Coaster** (Express Pass).

Toon Lagoon

Island of Adventure's sparkly, lighthearted cartoon-themed **Toon Lagoon** (☉9am-6pm, hours vary) transports visitors to the days when lazy weekends included nothing more than

☑ **Top Tips**

▶ Head to the Wizarding World of Harry Potter – Hogsmeade's Harry Potter and the Forbidden Journey ride when the park gates open, as lines can be hours long and it doesn't offer Express Pass access. Guests of some Universal Orlando Resort hotels can enter one hour early.

▶ Comic-book characters patrol Marvel Super Hero Island; check your map for scheduled meet-and-greet times.

✗ **Take a Break**

Pick up a Hog's Head Brew at Hog's Head Pub (p76) and sip it on the waterside patio out back.

In the Lost Continent, the Mystic Fountain banters sassily, soaking children with its waterspout – relax with hummus and kebabs from the walk-up Doc Sugrue's next door and watch the silly antics.

mornings watching Popeye and afternoons playing in the sprinkler. This is where you'll find most of Universal's water attractions, including **Popeye and Bluto's Bilge-Rat Barges** (Express Pass), a favorite river rafting ride for old-school, family-friendly, silly soaking fun; and **Dudley Do-Right's Ripsaw Falls** (Express Pass), a classic with a short but steep splash down into the water.

Seuss Landing

Anyone who has fallen asleep to the reading of *Green Eggs and Ham* or learned to read with *Sam I Am* knows the world of Dr Seuss: the fanciful creatures, the lyrical names, the rhyming stories. **Seuss Landing** (⊙9am-

6pm, hours vary), realized in magnificently designed three-dimensional form, is Dr Seuss' imagination. The Lorax guards his truffula trees; Thing One and Thing Two make trouble; and creatures from all kinds of Seuss favorites adorn the shops and the rides.

The Incredible Hulk Coaster

Follow the screams to this massive loop-dee-loop coaster just as you walk into the park. There's no clickity clackity building of suspense on this beast – you climb in, buckle up, and zoom, off you launch, from zero to 67mph. Climb up 150ft and fly down through a zero-gravity roll. It was reopened in 2016 with 'enhancements' including a new vehicle and a hi-tech scientific

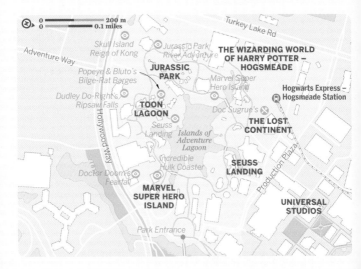

Understand

Top Tips for Visiting the Wizarding World

Get an early start *Harry Potter* attractions open one hour early for guests at four (of the five) on-site hotels. Otherwise, arrive at least 30 minutes before the gates open to the general public, and do not dawdle.

Buy a park-to-park ticket This allows you to ride the Hogwarts Express between Diagon Alley and Hogsmeade.

Strategize Head to Hogsmeade (p65) on one morning – hit Harry Potter and the Forbidden Journey, Dragon Challenge, Flight of the Hippogriff, then shops and restaurants. The other morning, zip straight to Diagon Alley (p61), hop on Escape from Gringotts, and then explore at leisure. There is an Ollivander's Wand Shop in both parks – make this your first stop on one of the two days.

Visit during low season Early September, early November and May see the lightest crowds. Don't go from Christmas through early January, March, April or summer.

Take advantage of Universal's 'return time' tickets If the Wizarding World reaches capacity (usually after 10:30am), it only allows new guests to enter once others have left – this electronic ticket allows you to enjoy other attractions and return for entry within a specific window of time. Look for the blue banner directing you to the easy-to-use kiosks.

facility centered around a 'Gamma Core' as the entrance.

Doctor Doom's Fearfall

You've seen rides like this at county fairs, but this one is a bit different. Rather than slowly working your way up the tower, this one blasts you over 150ft up in the air (apparently using more thrust than a 747 jet engine) and slams you free-fall down. If you don't have an Express Pass and the wait time stretches beyond 15 minutes,

come back later – it's fun, but not worth a long wait.

Skull Island Reign of Kong

Head off on one of the park's newest **rides** (⊙9am-6pm, hours vary) – on a 3D simulated, 1930s-style, volunteer expedition on 'off-road' terrain. Witness natives, prehistoric predators and fight to survive. Enter Kong, the colossal ape. Friend or foe? (We won't spoil this one.) Suffice to say, not for littlies.

Vineland Rd

Vineland Rd

Turkey Lake Rd

11

10

8

Woody
Woodpecker's
KidZone

San
Francisco 4

16

3

Major Blvd

27

31

19 24

26

22

15

Hollywood

5

**Universal
Studios**

P

Lost
Continent

33

17

28

2

13 18

23

**Islands of
Adventure**

9

6 Hollywood Drive-In Golf

29

7

14

P

S Kirkman Rd

Hollywood Way

30 20

32

25

12

Universal Blvd

Adventure Way

Turkey Lake Rd

S Kirkman Rd

For reviews see

◉ Top Sights	p60
◎ Sights	p69
✕ Eating	p71
🍷 Drinking	p75
✦ Entertainment	p76

Volcano Bay 1

International Dr

4

N 0 — 500 m
0 — 0.25 miles

Volcano Bay

Sights

Volcano Bay
AREA

1 ◎ Map p68, A5

Universal Resort's third theme park – a water park – launched in 2017. Modeled on a Pacific island, the tropical oasis' main feature is a colossal volcano through and down whichrun watery thrills and spills. Among the 18 attractions are winding rivers with family raft rides, pools and slides, but the main attraction is the Ko'okiri Body Plunge. At a hair-raising 125ft, it's the tallest trap-door body plunge ride in North America. (www.universalorlando.com; 6000 Universal Blvd, Universal Resort; ⊙from 9am, closing hours vary)

Lost Continent
AREA

2 ◎ Map p68, B3

Magic and myth from across the seas and the pages of fantasy books inspire this mystical corner of the park. Here you'll find dragons and unicorns, psychic readings and fortune-tellers. And don't be startled if that fountain talks to you as you walk past. The **Mystic Fountain** banters sassily, soaking children with its waterspouts when they least expect it and engaging them in silly conversation. (www.universal orlando.com; Islands of Adventure; theme-park admission required; ⊙9am-6pm, hours vary; 🚻; 🚌 Lynx 21, 37 or 40)

Local Life
Halloween Horror Nights

If you're in Orlando late September through October, try to snag a ticket to **Halloween Horror Nights** (www.halloweenhorrornights.com/orlando; Universal Studios; $70-81, plus theme-park admission; ⏲select nights Sep & Oct; 🚍Lynx 21, 37, or 40) for magnificently spooky haunted houses, gory thrills and over-the-top Halloween shows. Goblins, monsters and mummies roaming the streets, creeping up behind you, and remember, this is Universal, not Disney. It isn't Mickey-coated scares, and parents should think carefully before bringing children 13 and under.

Woody Woodpecker's KidZone　　AREA

3　◉　Map p68, C2

Kid-friendly shows and rides, a fantastic water-play area and supercool foam-ball cannons – it rivals Islands of Adventure's Seuss Landing (p66) as a Universal favorite of the eight-and-under crowd. (www.universalorlando.com; Universal Studios; theme-park admission required; ⏲from 9am; 🚍Lynx 21, 37 or 40)

San Francisco　　AREA

4　◉　Map p68, B2

San Francisco, themed heavily around the city as the site of the massive 1906 earthquake and the inspiration behind the 1974 film *Earthquake,* is home to Chez Alcatraz (p75), a tiny and pleasant outdoor bar in Fisherman's Wharf; Lombard's (p73), one of the park's two restaurants that accept reservations; and a couple of outdoor shows. (www.universalorlando.com; Universal Studios; theme-park admission required; ⏲from 9am; 🚻; 🚍Lynx 21, 37 or 40)

Hollywood　　AREA

5　◉　Map p68, C2

With glorious 3D film footage, live action stunts and 4D special effects, **Terminator 2: 3-D** (Express Pass) is complete sensory overload – delicious fun for some, overwhelming and scary for others. (www.universalorlando.com; Universal Studios; theme-park admission required; ⏲from 9am; 🚍Lynx 21, 37 or 40)

Hollywood Drive-In Golf　　MINIGOLF

6　◉　Map p68, C3

Putt through a flying saucer at the sci-fi-themed Invader from Planet Putt course; opt for haunted house shenanigans at the Haunting of Ghostly Greens course; or try both. Best at dark, when the LED special-effects lighting enhances the spooky thrills and silly twists. (📞407-802-4848; www.hollywooddriveingolf.com; CityWalk; adult/child 18-holes $16/14, 36-holes $29/25; ⏲9am-2am; 🚻; 🚍Lynx 21, 37 or 40, 🚇Universal)

Eating

Three Broomsticks
BRITISH $

7 Map p68, A3

Fast-food-styled British fare inspired by Harry Potter, with cottage (shepherd's) pie and Cornish pasties, and rustic wooden bench seating. There's plenty of outdoor seating out back, too, by the river. (www.universalorlando.com; Islands of Adventure; mains $12-17, theme-park admission required; ⏰9am-park closing; 🚶; 🚌Lynx 21, 37 or 40)

Mama Della's Ristorante
ITALIAN $$

8 Map p68, D1

Charming, cozy and friendly, with vintage wallpaper, dark wood and several rooms with romantic nooks. You really do feel like you're a welcomed guest at a private home nestled in Italy. Strolling musicians entertain tableside and the simple Italian fare is both fresh and excellent; the service is efficient but relaxed. (📞407-503-3463; www.universalorlando.com; 5601 Universal Blvd, Loews Portofino Bay Hotel; mains $10-22; ⏰5:30-11pm; 🍴🚶; ⛴Universal)

Toothsome Chocolate Emporium & Savory Feast Kitchen
INTERNATIONAL $

9 Map p68, B3

A delightfully quirky steampunk-meets-Willy-Wonka experience. Oh, and did we mention chocolate? If this description doesn't make sense, it isn't meant to, for that would spoil the surprise. Follow your nose here – head behind the smokestacks and into a world of chocolatey wonder with gadgets, gizmos and the 'creator,' Prof Dr Penelope Tibeaux-Tinker Toothsome. (http://stayinguniversal.com/menus/toothsome-chocolate-emporium-menu/; City Walk; ⏰11am-11pm Sun-Thu, 11am-11:30pm Fri & Sat)

Leaky Cauldron
BRITISH $

10 Map p68, B1

Wizard servers in marvelous Harry Potter surrounds with classic English breakfasts, shepherd's pie, Guinness beef stew and sticky toffee pudding.

 Top Tip

Wizarding Wands

Wands at Wizarding World come in two varieties, interactive ($48) and noninteractive ($40). Interactive wands can be used in both Diagon Alley and Hogsmeade to activate magical windows and displays. Make it rain down on an umbrella, illuminate lanterns, watch the marionettes dance. They can be a bit touchy to get used to – use small, gentle movements, and if you have trouble, ask a nearby wizard for help. Gold medallions on the ground indicate spots where and how you can cast spells, and each wand comes with a map. Some secret spell locations aren't marked at all. Hint: secret spells respond to a triangle swoop.

You order fast-food style and the food is brought to your table – refectory of course, à la Potteresque boarding-school experience. (www.universalorlando.com; Universal Studios; mains $8-15, theme-park admission required; ⏱8am-park closing; 🚌Lynx 21, 37 or 40)

Florean Fortescue's Ice-Cream Parlour
ICE CREAM $

11 Map p68, B1

In *Harry Potter and the Prisoner of Azkaban,* young Harry spends several weeks living at the Leaky Cauldron and Florean Fortescue gives him free ice cream whenever he pops into her store. Her bright and charming shop, just across from the fire-spewing dragon on top of Gringotts Bank, is now open to muggles – bizarre and delectable flavors include Butterbeer, sticky toffee pudding and clotted cream, as well as pumpkin juice. (www.universalorlandoresort.com; Diagon Alley, Universal Studios; ice cream $4-8, theme-park admission required; ⏱park opening-1hr before park closing; 🚌Lynx 21, 37 or 40)

Emeril's Tchoup Chop
SEAFOOD $$$

12 Map p68, C4

Island-inspired food, including plenty of seafood and Asian accents, prepared with the freshest ingredients. With stunning decor (massive orange and yellow lighting) and a more mellow ambience, this is one of the best sit-down meals at the Universal Orlando Resort. (📞407-503-2467; www.emerilsrestaurants.com; 6300 Hollywood Way, Loews Royal Pacific Resort; mains $24-36; ⏱11:30am-2:30pm & 5-10pm; 🚌Universal)

Cowfish
AMERICAN $$

13 Map p68, C3

'Burgushi'...this is something you'd only find in the US. Surely. Yes, a fusion between a burger and sushi. In reality, it's more sushi with a burger component rather than fusion cuisine. But it's good. Cowfish (getting the idea, here?) is a mighty popular spot with a fabulous bar. (📞407-224-3663; www.universalorlando.com; CityWalk, Universal Resort; mains $15-23; ⏱10:30am-11pm Sun-Thu, to midnight Fri & Sat)

Confisco Grille & Backwater Bar
AMERICAN $

14 Map p68, B3

Under-the-radar and often overlooked, the recommended Confisco Grille has outdoor seating, freshly made hummus, tasty wood-oven pizzas and a full bar. (📞407-224-4012; www.universalorlando.com; Islands of Adventure; mains $6-22, theme-park admission required; ⏱11am-4pm; 🍴♿; 🚌Lynx 21, 37 or 40)

Mel's Drive-In
BURGERS $

15 Map p68, C2

Based on the movie *American Graffiti*, this rockin' rollin' joint features classic cars and performing bands outside, '50s-diner style inside. This is a fast-food eatery, not very different really from your standard well-known burger joint, but it's a lot more fun!

The Incredible Hulk Coaster (p66), Islands of Adventure

(www.universalorlando.com; Universal Studios; mains $10-14, theme-park admission required; ⏰11am-park closing; 🚹; 🚌Lynx 21, 37 or 40, 🚤Universal)

Lombard's Seafood Grille
SEAFOOD $$

16 🍴 Map p68, B2

A more upmarket experience (and good for older folk). Features oriental rugs, a huge fish tank and a solid seafood menu. It's a calming respite from Universal Orlando's energy. (📞407-224-3613, 407-224-6401; www.universalorlando.com; Universal Studios; mains $15-28, theme-park admission required; ⏰11am-park closing; 📶🚹; 🚌Lynx 21, 37 or 40)

NBC Sports Grill & Brew
AMERICAN $$

17 🍴 Map p68, C3

In their own PR terms 'a game changer.' This massive sports grill and brew brings on all the sporting analogies. Not only is there a 120ft-wide screen (playing the greatest moments in NBC sports history), but another 100 smaller screens showing live coverage of all types of games, plus more than 100 beers, from craft to regional brews. (www.universalorlando.com; City Walk, Universal Orlando Resort; mains $14-40; ⏰11am-1:30am)

Bob Marley – A Tribute to Freedom
JAMAICAN $$

18 Map p68, C3

Jerk-spiced chicken, monk stew and veggie patties with yucca fries served in a replica of the reggae master's Jamaican home. There's live reggae in the courtyard every evening, and after 9pm you must be 21 to enter. (☏407-224-3663; www.universalorlando.com; CityWalk; mains $15-18; ⏰4pm-2am; ☒Lynx 21, 37 or 40, ☻Universal)

Palm Restaurant
STEAK $$$

19 Map p68, C2

The original Palm opened in New York City in 1926 and, though there are now more than 30 locations, it remains a family-owned bedrock American steakhouse, albeit up there in the price stakes, too. Classic cocktails, a steady din and big plates of steak, lobster and Italian fare. (☏407-503-7256; www.thepalm.com; 5800 Universal Studios Blvd, Hard Rock Hotel; mains $38-59; ⏰5-10pm; ☻Universal)

Orchid Court Sushi Bar
JAPANESE $$

20 Map p68, C4

This small, informal sushi bar oozes calm inside the light-and-airy, glass-enclosed lobby of the Royal Pacific Resort, and is decked out with cushioned couches and chairs. Try the moonstone lychetini (or whatever 'tini' they have going; $15). It's also open for breakfast. (☏407-503-3000; www.universalorlando.com; 6300 Hollywood Way, Loews Royal Pacific Resort; sushi $5-16, mains $13-20; ⏰6-11am & 5-11pm; ☒; ☻Universal)

Hard Rock Café
AMERICAN $$

21 Map p68, C3

Excellent burgers and a rock 'n' roll theme make this a fan favorite. Plus it's open for breakfast – handy for a prepark carbo-fill. Reservations not accepted, but you can ring ahead for 'priority seating,' meaning that if there's a wait, you can queue-jump (but are not guaranteed a seat). (☏407-351-7625; www.hardrock.com/cafes/orlando; CityWalk; mains $13-27; ⏰8:30am-midnight; ☒; ☒Lynx 21, 37 or 40, ☻Universal)

Finnegan's Bar & Grill
PUB FOOD $$

22 Map p68, B2

An Irish pub with live acoustic music plopped into the streets of New York. Serves Cornish pasties and Scotch eggs, as well as Harp, Bass and Guinness on tap. Annoyingly (as with many establishments, it seems), the prices are not shown on the outside menu. (☏407-224-3613; www.universalorlando.com; Universal Studios; mains $10-23, theme-park admission required; ⏰11am-park closing; ☒☒; ☒Lynx 21, 37 or 40)

Mythos Restaurant
MEDITERRANEAN $$

23 Map p68, B3

Housed in an ornate underwater grotto with giant windows and running water and overlooking a lake, this is a more upmarket experience and the best of the selection. Menu changes seasonally but you can chomp on anything from pad thai noodles to risotto. (☎407-224-4012, 407-224-4534; www.universalorlando.com; Islands of Adventure; mains $14-23, theme-park admission required; ⏱11am-3pm; 🖢; 🚌Lynx 21, 37 or 40)

Kitchen
AMERICAN $$$

24 🍽 Map p68, C2

Music paraphernalia and patio poolside dining. Come for flatbreads, steak and comfort food such as chicken potpie and roast chicken. Children can head to the Kids' Crib, which has bean-bag chairs, cartoons and toys, while parents dine in the big-people restaurant. Every night two characters visit tables. (☎407-503-2430; www.zloewshotels.com/hard-rock/dining/restaurant; 5800 Universal Blvd, Hard Rock Hotel; mains $15-40; ⏱7am-10pm Sun-Thu, to 11pm Fri & Sat; 🖢; 🚎Universal)

Drinking

Strong Water Tavern
BAR

25 🍺 Map p68, B4

This sophisticated rum and tapas bar will transport you to the Caribbean. Rum barrel lids are suspended overhead, and other wood accents transform this hotel bar into an atmospheric, stylish place. You can take a journey through different types of rum (there are more than 60 to

try) and a rum counsel is on hand to advise. (www.loewshotels.com/sapphire-falls-resort/dining/lounges; Loews Sapphire Falls Resort, Universal Orlando Resort; 🛜)

Velvet Bar
LOUNGE

26 🍺 Map p68, C2

Trendy and sleekly stylized, with hardwood floors, floor-to-ceiling windows, zebra-fabric chairs and excellent martinis. On the last Thursday of the month, it hosts Velvet Sessions, a rock 'n' roll cocktail party with themed drinks, finger food and a renowned musician (okay, it might not be Lady Gaga, but it will be someone who has had a name at some stage). (☎407-504-2588, tickets & info 407-503-2401; www.hardrockhotelorlando.com/orlando; 5800 Universal Blvd, Hard Rock Hotel; ⏱5pm-2am; 🚎Universal)

Chez Alcatraz
BAR

27 🍺 Map p68, B2

Frozen mojitos, flatbread and homemade potato chips on the waterfront at Fisherman's Wharf. With the sound of the boats jingling at the docks, views over the water to the *Simpsons*-themed Springfield, and Bruce the infamous shark from *Jaws* dangling as a photo-op, this little outdoor bar makes a pleasant spot to kick back and relax. (www.universalorlando.com; San Francisco, Universal Studios; theme-park admission required; ⏱11am-park closing; 🛜; 🚌Lynx 21, 37 or 40)

Hog's Head Pub
PUB

28 Map p68, A3

Butterbeer, frozen or frothy, real beer on tap, pumpkin cider and more. Keep an eye on that hog over the bar – he's more real than you think! If the lines at the Butterbeer carts outside are too long, head inside. Same thing, same price. (www.universalorlando.com; Islands of Adventure, Universal Studios; drinks $4-8, theme-park admission required; ⏲11am-park closing; ☒Lynx 21, 37 or 40)

Red Coconut Club
CLUB

This place (see 29 Map p68, C3) is meant to tap into a '50s Cuba, retro Polynesian and contemporary feel. It may be a melange, but it has a hip vibe, plus live bands, a martini bar and rooftop balcony. (☏407-224-4233; www.universalorlando.com; CityWalk; after 10pm $7; ⏲8pm-2am Sun-Thu, from 6pm Fri & Sat; ☒Lynx 21, 37 or 40, ☻Universal)

Local Life
CityWalk

Across the canal from the theme parks, and open to the public (for free), Universal's pedestrian mall entertainment district has themed restaurants, bars, a multiplex movie theater, miniature golf, shops and a fountain for kids to play in. Live music and mucho alcohol sum up the entertainment options here, particularly after 9pm, but there's a family-friendly vibe and several bars have decent food.

Pat O'Brien's
BAR

29 Map p68, C3

A replica of a bar of the same name in New Orleans, this has Cajun food (mains $8 to $17), dueling pianos and a pleasant outdoor patio. (☏407-224-2106; www.universalorlando.com; CityWalk; after 10pm $7; ⏲4pm-2am, piano bar from 5pm; ☒Lynx 21, 37 or 40, ☻Universal)

Jake's American Bar
BAR

30 Map p68, B4

Glide into this South Seas island experience where 'Jake', imaginary pilot of an island-hopper aircraft, runs this pleasant place. We don't want to overstress the theming here, and we're not talking *Gilligan's Island* though the 'pilot log book' menu (mains $13 to $17) is kind of fun. It is a stylish locale, worthy of the Royal Pacific.

Serves everything from beer flights to great snacks. Try the killer crab-cake sandwich ($16). (www.universal orlando.com; Loews Royal Pacific Resort, Universal Orlando Resort; ⏲11am-1:30am)

Entertainment

Universal's Cinematic Spectacular
CINEMA

31 Map p68, C2

This dramatic film tribute narrated by Morgan Freeman combines fireworks, a water and light show, and clips from movie classics projected on a massive screen over the lagoon. (☏dining reservations 407-224-7554; www.universalorlando.

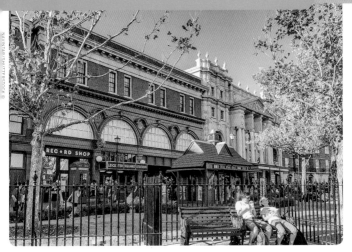

San Francisco area (p70), Universal Studios

com; Universal Studios; theme-park admission required; ⊘evenings, times vary; ⊞Lynx 21, 37 or 40)

Wantilan Luau   LUAU

32 ⭐ Map p68, C4

Pacific Island fire dancers shimmy and shake on stage while guests enjoy a tasty buffet of roast suckling pig, guava-barbecued short ribs and other Polynesian-influenced fare. The atmosphere is wonderfully casual and, like everything at Universal Orlando, this is simple unabashed silliness and fun. Unlimited mai tais, beer and wine are included in the price. (⌕407-503-3463; www.universalorlando.com; 6300

Hollywood Way, Loews Royal Pacific Resort; adult $70-76, child 3-9yr $35-40; ⊘6pm Sat; ⊛Universal)

Blue Man Group   PERFORMING ARTS

33 ⭐ Map p68, B3

Originally an off-Broadway phenomenon in 1991, this high-energy, comedy theatrical troupe at Universal Orlando Resort features all kinds of multisensory craziness – percussion 'instruments,' paintballs, marshmallows, modern dancing and general mayhem. (⌕407-258-3626; www.universalorlando.com; CityWalk; adult/child from $60/30; ⊘times vary; ⊞Lynx 21, 37 or 40, ⊛Universal)

Explore

International Drive

I-Drive is Orlando's tourist hub, packed with restaurants, bars, stores, accommodations and Orlando attractions. It parallels I-4 to its east, stretching 17 miles from Orlando Premium Outlets south to World Dr, just east of Walt Disney World®. The section between the convention center and Sand Lake Rd is a relatively pleasant walking district, and from Sand Lake Rd north it is Orlando tourism at full throttle.

The Sights in a Day

Spend your morning at **Sea Life** (p82) before the crowds arrive. On your way out, use your three-attraction pass to drop into nearby **Madame Tussauds** (p83) for some quick snaps with your favorite wax celebrities.

When you've had your fill of selfies, stroll along I-Drive and browse for kitschy souvenirs before stopping for a fun diner lunch at **Johnny Rockets** (p84).

Pop into **WonderWorks** (p81), for a few hours exploring the interactive exhibits before music and dinner at arty **Cafe Tu Tu Tango** (p84). Top off the evening with a circuit on the **Orlando Eye** (p82) and drinks at super-cool **Icebar** (p85).

 **Best of International Drive**

Eating
Johnny Rockets (p84)

Cafe Tu Tu Tango (p84)

Drinking & Nightlife
Icebar (p85)

Getting There

I-Ride Trolley (p143) Services International Dr, from south of SeaWorld north to the Universal Orlando Resort area.

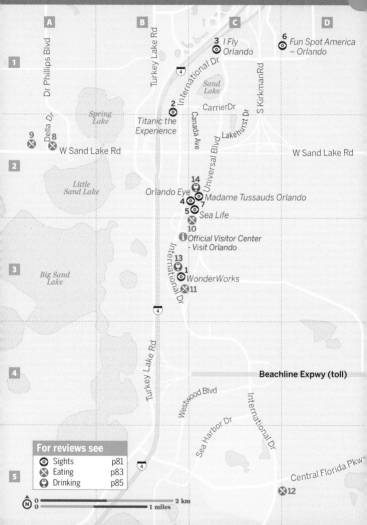

A1 Dr Phillips Blvd

B Turkey Lake Rd

3 I Fly Orlando

6 Fun Spot America – Orlando

S Kirkman Rd

International Dr

Sand Lake

Carrier Dr

2 Titanic the Experience

Spring Lake

Canada Ave

Lakehurst Dr

Universal Blvd

9
8
W Sand Lake Rd

W Sand Lake Rd

Little Sand Lake

14
Orlando Eye
4 **7** Madame Tussauds Orlando
5 Sea Life
10

Big Sand Lake

Official Visitor Center - Visit Orlando

13 **1**
International Dr
WonderWorks
11

Beachline Expwy (toll)

Turkey Lake Rd

Westwood Blvd

Sea Harbor Dr

International Dr

Central Florida Pkw

12

For reviews see
Sights		p81
Eating		p83
Drinking		p85

N
0 ——— 2 km
0 ——— 1 miles

INGUS KRUKLITIS/SHUTTERSTOCK ©

WonderWorks

Sights

WonderWorks
MUSEUM

1 ⊙ Map p80, C3

Housed in a hard-to-miss, upside-down building, this is yet another bright, loud, frenetic landmark trying to make its mark in Orlando. This one is a cross between a children's museum, a video arcade and an amusement park. Several stories of interactive exhibits offer high-speed, multisensory education. (☎407-351-8800; www.wonderworksonline.com; 9067 International Dr; adult/child 4-12yr $30/24; ☺9am-midnight; ⟦⟧; ⧠Lynx 8, 38, 42, ⧠I-Ride Trolley Red Line Stop 18 or Green Line Stop 10)

Titanic the Experience
MUSEUM

2 ⊙ Map p80, B1

Full-scale replicas of the doomed ship's interior and artifacts found at the bottom of the sea. Tour the galleries with guides in period dress or wander through on your own. Kids especially love the dramatic and realistic interpretation of history – each passenger receives a boarding pass, with the name of a real passenger, and at the end of the experience (once the ship has sunk) you learn your fate. (☎407-248-1166; www.titanicshipofdreams.com; 7324 International Dr; adult/child 6-11yr $22/16; ☺10am-6pm; ⟦⟧; ⧠Lynx 8, 42, ⧠I-Ride Trolley Red Line Stop 9)

Understand
Water Parks & Wildlife

Since the early 1990s, keeping dolphins, sea lions and whales in captivity for the purposes of public display and human interaction has become increasingly controversial. Animal welfare groups and marine scientists have come out against the practice, which is debilitating and stressful for these sensitive and complex creatures. As a result, dolphins and marine mammals kept in captivity often live much shorter lives than those in the wild. Visitors to Florida should be aware of the ethical issues surrounding some of the region's most popular attractions, particularly live shows featuring trained dolphins, sea lions or killer whales.

After the release of the 2013 documentary *Blackfish*, the treatment of captive orcas at **SeaWorld** came under intense scrutiny, and the park has seen falling visitor numbers and negative PR. They have since stopped displaying the whales at the San Diego park. According to media reports, the company plans to phase out orca shows in Orlando by 2019, but at the time of research, dolphin, sea lion and whale shows were continuing.

Aquatica, owned by SeaWorld, has no dolphin or whale shows, but does feature a tank of black-and-white Commerson's dolphins that are on display every two hours for feedings.

I Fly Orlando   ADVENTURE SPORTS

3 Map p80, C1

Think you might like to jump out of a moving plane? Or does the thought give you the heebie-jeebies? This indoor skydiving experience sends you soaring free-form in a vertical wind tunnel, giving you a taste of the real thing. (☏407-903-1150; www.iflyorlando. com; 6805 Visitors Cir; adult from $60; ☺10:30am-9pm Mon-Fri; 🚼)

Orlando Eye   AMUSEMENT PARK

4 Map p80, C2

Orlando has got everything else that goes up and down, so why not round and around? Opened in 2017, the Eye is International Drive's latest landmark. Orlando is flat, but a trip in this, especially at night, affords views of theme parks and the greater area. Check ahead as it sometimes closes for private events. (www.officialorlandoeye.com; I-Drive 360, 8401 International Dr; from $20; ☺10am-10pm Sun-Thu, to midnight Fri & Sat)

Sea Life   AQUARIUM

5 Map p80, C2

One of a chain that operates around the world, Sea Life is another wildlife showcase of the underwater world variety. It's divided into many themes; the 360-degree glass tunnel is the highly promoted centerpiece. It has an educative, sustainable line to its exhibits, including talks and feeding sessions. Online prices are $5 less per person. Combination tickets are available with the Orlando Eye and Madame Tussauds. (☏866-622-0607; www.visitsealife/orlando; 8449 International Dr; adult/child $25/20; ⏱10am-9pm)

Fun Spot America – Orlando
AMUSEMENT PARK

6 Map p80, D1

County-fair-like amusement park, with go-carts, kiddy rides, a wooden roller coaster and more. There's a small section called 'Gator Spot' with around 100 young 'gators, including a rare white species. It doesn't have the clever theming or simulated masterpieces of the bigger parks and it's pretty dated, but the lines aren't hours long. (☏407-363-3867; http://fun-spot.com; 5700 Fun Spot Way; admission free, unlimited all-day rides adult/child under 54in $46/40, per ride $3-9; ⏱10am-midnight; 🚍I-Ride Trolley Red Line Stop 1, 2)

Madame Tussauds Orlando
MUSEUM

7 Map p80, C2

Kitsch, celebrity-filled and featuring everyone from historic and cultural figures to current film icons. Part of the Merlin Entertainment section with the Orlando Eye and Sea Life, it's selfie heaven. (☏866-630-8315; www.madametussauds.com/orlando; 8387 International Dr; from $20; 🚍I-Ride Trolley Red Line 14, Green Line 8)

Eating

Slate
AMERICAN $$

8 🍴 Map p80, A2

One of Orlando's newest and trendiest places, it's buzzy, noisy and draws a chatty crowd after crusty pizza (straight from the large, copper oven) or contemporary dishes from brisket to diver scallops. There are several seating areas, from a communal table to the wood room, a verandah-style space with a fireplace. (☏407-500-7528; www.slateorlando.com; 8323 W Sand Lake Rd, Restaurant Row; mains $14-38; ⏱11am-12:30pm & 5-10pm Mon-Fri, 10:30-3pm & 5-11pm Sat, 10:30-3pm & 5-9pm Sun)

Urbain 40
AMERICAN $$

9 🍴 Map p80, A2

Tap into your inner classy selves and transport yourself back to the 1940s, where classic martinis were downed

Local Life
Restaurant Row

The 5-mile stretch of Sand Lake Rd from I-4 (at Whole Foods) west to Apopka-Vineland Rd and including Dr Philips Blvd, is known as **Restaurant Row**. Here you'll find a concentration of restaurants and high-end chains more popular with locals than tourists, with everything from wine bars to cigar bars, sushi to burgers.

like water by besuited clients who sat on blue leather bar stools. This stunning old-style American brasserie manages to re-create this (without contrivance) and serves up great cuisine as well as ambience. Do not miss the char-roasted mussels ($12). (📞407-872-2640; http://urbain40.com/; 8000 Via Dellagio Way, Restaurant Row)

Cafe Tu Tu Tango
TAPAS $$

10 Map p80, C3

Local artwork, all for sale, crams the adobe-style walls of this bright, fun eatery. It's action packed with music and performers. Or you can relax on

 Top Tip
Shopping
The areas around the theme parks and lining the highways are defined by souvenirs, kitschy must-haves, outlet shopping and indoor malls with all the national chains.

Orlando Premium Outlets has all the usual discount-mall suspects with branches on **International Dr** (📞407-352-9600; www.premiumoutlets. com/outlet/orlando-international; 4951 International Dr; 🕙10am-11pm Mon-Sat, to 9pm Sun; 🚌Lynx 8 or 42, 🚌I-Ride Trolley Red Line 1) and **Vineland Ave** (📞407-238-7787; www.premiumoutlets. com/outlet/orlando-vineland; 8200 Vineland Ave; 🕙10am-11pm Mon-Fri, to 9pm Sun; 🚌I-Ride Trolley Red Line 38).

the patio with cajun chicken egg rolls and a plate of alligator bites, washed down with a pitcher of sangria. Share plates are 'globally inspired' with Asian and Mediterranean influences. Great for Sunday brunch. (📞407-248-2222; www.cafetututango.com; 8625 International Dr; share plates $8-14; 🕙11:30am-midnight Mon-Thu, to 1am Fri & Sat, 10am-11pm Sun)

Johnny Rockets
DINER $

11 Map p80, B3

Located in the Pointe Orlando on International Dr, this is straight out of *Happy Days*, with red vinyl seating, lots of chrome and flip-style jukeboxes on the tables; the Fonz would feel right at home at this burger-joint chain. (📞407-903-0762; www.johnnyrock ets.com; 9101 International Dr, No 1100; mains $7-11; 🕙11am-10pm Sun-Thu, to 11pm Fri & Sat; 👶; 🚌Red Line 20)

Thai Thani
THAI $$

12 Map p80, D5

A friendly, cool and quiet restaurant stuck out on its own in a mall (handy if you're staying near SeaWorld), with gilded Thai decor and some tables with traditional floor seating. Good food, but watered-down spice – for a kick, ask for level 5 and above. (📞407-239-9733; www.thaithani.net; 11025 International Dr; mains $9-22; 🕙11:30am-11pm; 👶; 🚌I-Ride Trolley Red Line)

GOSKOVA TATIANA/SHUTTERSTOCK ©

Drinking

Icebar   BAR

13 📍 Map p80, B3

More classic Orlando gimmicky fun. Step into the 22ºF (-5ºC) ice house, sit on the ice seat, admire the ice carvings, sip the icy drinks. Coat and gloves are provided at the door (or upgrade to the photogenic faux fur for $10), and the fire room, bathrooms and other areas of the bar are kept at normal temperature.

Adults over 21 welcome anytime; folks aged between eight and 20 are allowed between 7pm and 9pm only. (☑407-426-7555; www.icebarorlando.com; 8967 International Dr; entry at door/advance online $20/15; ⏰5pm-midnight Mon-Wed, to 1am Thu, to 2am Fri-Sun; 🚌I-Trolley Red Line Stop 18 or Green Line Stop 10)

Tin Roof   BAR

14 📍 Map p80, C2

The famous live-music joint that encourages performances of all standards. It's part of the I-Drive 360 complex (think the Orlando Eye and more). Serves up reasonable (bordering on very nice) junk food – burgers, mac 'n' cheese – and things that will fuel you until the wee hours. (☑407-270-7926; www.tinrooforlando.com; 8371 International Dr, I-Drive 360; ⏰11am-2am)

Explore

Downtown Orlando

Orlando has a lot to offer: lovely tree-lined neighborhoods; a rich performing arts and museum scene; several fantastic gardens and nature preserves; fabulous cuisine; and is delightfully devoid of manic crowds. So come down off the coasters to explore the quieter, gentler side of the city. You may be surprised to find that you enjoy the theme parks all that much more as a result.

The Sights in a Day

🔅 You don't need a jam-packed itinerary to cover the sights of downtown Orlando – this is a good day for a leisurely and lazy start. Linger over brunch at **Dexters of Thornton Park** (p93) and stroll around Thornton Park. Remodeled bungalows line the narrow brick streets, giant Spanish oak weave their gnarly branches into natural green canopies, and urban-hip families gather at the lakeside playground.

🔅 Walk the lake path at **Lake Eola Park** (p91) and relax with a book or take in some local history at **Orange County Regional History Center** (p91).

🌙 Head to the Westin Grand Bohemian, one of the city's most upmarket hotels, for happy hour and jazz at the **Bösendorfer Lounge** (p94), head to **Stubborn Mule** (p92) for dinner, then catch an improv performance at **SAK Comedy Lab** (p95) or live music at the **Beacham** (p95).

For a local's night out in Downtown Orlando, see p88.

🔍 Local Life

A Night Out in Downtown Orlando (p88)

Getting There

🚌 **Lymmo** (www.golynx.com; free; ⏱6am-10pm Mon-Thu, to midnight Fri, 10am-midnight Sat, to 10pm Sun) circles downtown Orlando for free with stops near Lynx Central Station, near SunRail's Church St Station, at Central and Magnolia, Jefferson and Magnolia and outside the Westin Grand Bohemian.

🚆 **Rail** Sunrail (www.sunrail.com), Orlando's commuter rail train, runs north–south. It doesn't stop at or near any theme parks. In addition to the downtown station, Amtrak (p142) serves Winter Park, Kissimmee and Winter Haven (home to Legoland).

Local Life
A Night Out in Downtown Orlando

Night is what downtown Orlando does best. Music filters out from the city's many bars, sidewalk tables invite lazy lingering over cocktails, and there's a rowdy college-town vibe as the night wears on. This local crawl takes you beyond the drink-pounding happy-hour specials into some of the city's best low-key favorites.

....

❶ Cocktails at the Courtesy

Start your crawl with a Moscow Mule at the **Courtesy Bar** (☏407-450-2041; www.thecourtesybar.com; 114 N Orange Ave, Downtown; drinks from $5; ⊗7pm-2am Mon & Sat, 5pm-2am Tue-Fri, 3pm-2am Sun), housed in a historic Orlando space with brick walls and Jefferson filament bulbs. This little old-school cocktail bar serves up high-quality

spirits with fresh and quirky artisan twists such as Himalayan pink salt, fresh honeydew juice and, rather oddly, dandelion-eucalyptus tincture. There's an excellent selection of beer and wine, $4 happy-hour specials, and Peter Gabriel, The Cure and indie folk crank unobtrusively from the iPod.

❷ Farm-to-Table Dinner

There's a festive vibe to dusk in downtown Orlando – music seeps out from pubs, business folk kick back over happy-hour beers, and outdoor bars bustle. Head to Rusty Spoon (p92), which serves pub classics in an airy building with a trendy urban vibe.

❸ Take in a Play

Catch a performance at the venerable **Mad Cow Theatre** (☏ 407-297-8788; www.madcowtheatre.com; 54 W Church, Downtown; tickets from $26). This intimate regional playhouse regularly earns rave reviews for its stagings of local playwrights, theater classics such as *Cat on a Hot Tin Roof,* and Broadway hits.

❹ Rooftop Terrace Drinks

The island-inspired Latitudes (p94), a rooftop bar with tiki lanterns and city views, is always hopping and a pleasant place to enjoy the Florida night skies. Alternatively, opt for the 'champagne experience' and have a whirl on the Orlando Eye for great views of the city lights.

❺ Live Music

Finish the night at Tanqueray's (p94), an unpretentious little underground haunt. It can get smoky and loud, but this little dive plays some of the best live local music in town.

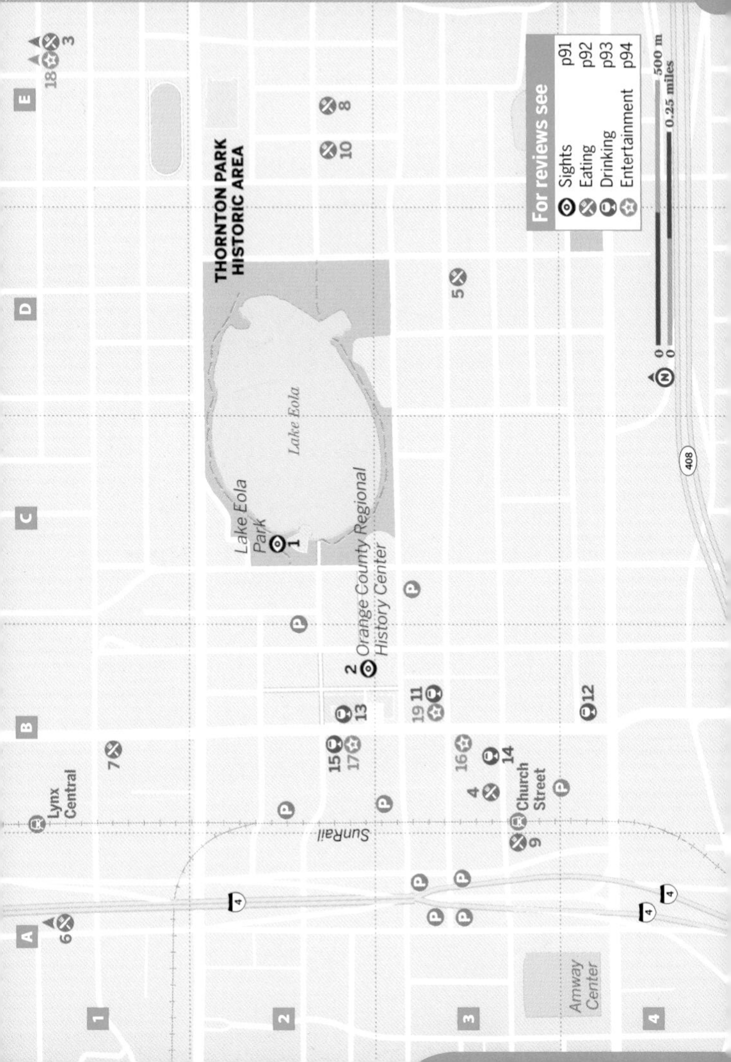
A
B
C
D
E
1
2
3
4
Lynx Central
7
6
18
3
THORNTON PARK HISTORIC AREA
Lake Eola Park
1
Lake Eola
Orange County Regional History Center
2
15
17
13
19
11
16
14
4
Church Street
9
SunRail
12
5
10
8
Amway Center
408
4
For reviews see
Sights p91
Eating p92
Drinking p93
Entertainment p94
0
500 m
0
0.25 miles

Orange County Regional History Center

Sights

Lake Eola Park   PARK

1  Map p90, C2

Pretty and shaded, this little city park sits between downtown Orlando and Thornton Park. A paved sidewalk circles the water, there's a waterfront playground and you can rent swan paddleboats. On Saturday mornings, the park is home to the Orlando Farmers Market (p94). (195 N Rosalind Ave; ⏰6am–midnight; 👶)

Orange County Regional History Center   MUSEUM

2  Map p90, B2

Orlando before Disney? Permanent exhibits cover prehistoric Florida, European exploration, race relations and citrus production, with a re-created pioneer home and 1927 courtroom. (📞407-836-8500; www.thehistorycenter. org; 65 E Central Blvd, Downtown; adult/child 5-12yr $8/6; ⏰10am-5pm Mon-Sat, from noon Sun; 👶)

Eating

Dandelion Communitea Café
VEGETARIAN $

3 Map p90, E1

Unabashedly crunchy and definitively organic, this pillar of the sprouts and tempeh and green-tea dining scene serves up creative and excellent plant-based fare in a refurbished old house that invites folks to sit down and hang out. (☏407-362-1864; www.dandelion communitea.com; 618 N Thornton Ave, Thornton Park; mains $10-14; ☉11am-10pm Mon-Sat, to 5pm Sun; 🖉🚻)

Rusty Spoon
AMERICAN $$

4 Map p90, B3

Airy, handsome and inviting, with a brick wall covered in giant photos of farm animals, a trendy urban vibe and an emphasis on simply prepared, locally sourced produce. Kind of pub

classics with delightful (and much more sophisticated) twists. If it's on the menu, don't bypass the chocolate 'smores dessert. (We say no more.) (☏407-401-8811; www.therustyspoon.com; 55 W Church St, Downtown; mains $15-31; ☉11am-3pm Mon-Fri, 5-11pm Sun-Thu, to 11pm Fri & Sat; 🖉)

Stubborn Mule
MODERN AMERICAN $$

5 Map p90, D3

A trendy and very popular gastropub that serves handcrafted cocktails with flair (yes, plenty of mules) and good ol' locally sourced, delicious food that's nothing but contemporary. It serves up the likes of polenta cakes and smoked Gouda grits and roasted winter vegetables. It's the new kid on the block and one definitely worth visiting. (www.thestubbornmuleorlando. com; 100 S Eola Drive, Suite 103, Downtown; mains $19-28; ☉11am-11pm Tue-Sat, 11am-9pm Sun)

K Restaurant
AMERICAN $$$

6 Map p90, A1

Chef and owner Kevin Fonzo, one of Orlando's most celebrated and established field-to-fork foodie stars, earns local and national accolades year after year, but this neighborhood favorite remains wonderfully unassuming. There's a wraparound porch, and a lovely little terrace, and herbs and vegetables come from the on-site garden. (☏407-872-2332; www.krestaurant.net; 1710 Edgewater Dr, College Park; mains

$18-40; ⏰5-9pm Mon-Thu, 5:30-10pm Fri & Sat, 5:30-8pm Sun; ✏)

DoveCote

FRENCH $$

7 Map p90, B1

One of the hottest tickets in Orlando sits tidily within the city's Bank of America building. It's an all-things-to-all-people kind of spot with a brasserie and a coffee stop, plus plenty of cocktails. 'Comfort French' is often used to describe the cuisine. (http://dovecoteorlando.com/; 390 N Orange Ave, Ste 110; lunch mains $12-24, dinner mains $16-30; ⏰11:30am-2:30pm & 5:30-10pm)

Dexters of Thornton Park

AMERICAN $$

8 Map p90, E2

Neighborhood restaurant with outdoor seating and a popular daily brunch that includes interesting twists on breakfast mainstays, including pepper-jack grits. Many diners say they have the best shrimp and grits in town. Sip on a selection of fruity mimosas including peach, mango and pineapple. (📞407-648-2777; www.dextersorlando.com; 808 E Washington St, Thornton Park; mains $10-25; ⏰7am-10pm Mon-Wed, 7am-11pm Thu & Fri, 11am-2am Sat, 10am-10pm Sun)

Hamburger Mary's

BURGERS $$

9 Map p90, A3

Downtown high-energy diner specializing in over-the-top burgers with sweet-potato fries and serious cocktails. There's a Broadway Brunch with show tunes, drag shows and all kinds of interactive entertainment. (📞321-319-0600; www.hamburgermarys.com; 110 W Church St, Downtown; mains $10-16; ⏰11am-10pm Sun & Mon, 11am-10:30pm Tue-Thu, 11am-11:30pm Fri & Sat)

Benjamin French Bakery

BAKERY $

10 Map p90, E2

Bright little French bakery featuring rustic sandwiches, salads and omelets. Your best bet, though, is a pastry and coffee to go. Try the crusty homemade baguette or a croissant of whatever flavor they've made that day. (📞407-797-2293; www.benjaminfrenchbakery.com; 716 E Washington St, Thornton Park; pastries $4, mains $3-9; ⏰8am-6pm)

Drinking

Hanson's Shoe Repair

COCKTAIL BAR

11 🍸 Map p90, B3

In a city saturated with over-the-top theming from Beauty and the Beast to Harry Potter, it shouldn't be surprising that you can walk from 21st-century Downtown Orlando into a Prohibition-era speakeasy, complete with historically accurate cocktails and a secret password for entry. To get in, call for the password. (📞407-476-9446; www.facebook.com/hansonsshoerepair/; 3rd fl, 27 E Pine St, Downtown; cocktails $12; ⏰8pm-2am Tue-Thu & Sat, from 7pm Fri)

Local Life
Orlando Farmers Market
This boho, little **weekend market** (www.orlandofarmersmarket.com; Lake Eola; ⊙10am-4pm Sun) on the shores of Lake Eola makes a lovely place to while away a Sunday. Peruse the booths of local crafts and area produce, pop into the Raw Juice tent for a Mean Green Smoothie, chow down on a decadedly delicious sweet or savory crepe, and chill to live music in the beer garden. Though it's technically a farmers market, you'll find more craft and food vendors than lettuce and berries.

Bösendorfer Lounge
LOUNGE

12 Map p90, B4

Zebra-fabric chairs, gilded mirrors, massive black pillars and marble floors ooze pomp and elegance. This hotel bar is popular for after-work drinks and the lounge picks up with live jazz at 7pm. The name stems from the lounge's rare Bösendorfer piano. (☎407-313-9000; www.grandbohemianhotel. com; 325 S Orange Ave, Westin Grand Bohemian; ⊙11am-2am)

Woods
COCKTAIL BAR

13 Map p90, B2

Craft cocktails and craft beers hidden in a cozy, smoke-free, 2nd-floor setting (in the historic Rose Building), with exposed brick, a tree-trunk bar and an earthy feel. (☎407-203-1114; www. thewoodsorlando.com; 49 N Orange Ave,

Downtown; cocktails $12; ⊙5pm-2am Mon-Fri, from 7pm Sat, 4pm-midnight Sun)

Latitudes
BAR

14 Map p90, B3

An Orlando classic, the island-inspired Latitudes, a rooftop bar with tiki lanterns and city views, is always hopping. You have to walk up past thumping bars on the first two floors to get here, but once up it's a pleasant place to enjoy the Florida night skies. (☎407-649-4270; www.churchstreetbars.com; 33 W Church St, Downtown; ⊙4:30pm-2am)

Independent Bar
CLUB

15 Map p90, B2

Known to locals as simply the 'I-Bar,' it's hip, crowded and loud, with DJs spinning underground dance and alternative rock into the wee hours. (☎407-839-0457; 68 N Orange Ave, Downtown; $10; ⊙10pm-3am Sun, Wed & Thu, from 9:30pm Fri & Sat)

Entertainment
Tanqueray's Downtown Orlando
LIVE MUSIC

16 Map p90, B3

A former bank vault, this underground smoky dive bar draws folks looking to hang out with friends over a beer. There's Guinness on tap, and you can catch local bands, usually reggae or blues, on the weekend. (☎407-649-8540; 100 S Orange Ave, Downtown; ⊙11am-2am Mon-Fri, 6pm-2am Sat & Sun)

CHRISTINA MAHESE/SHUTTERSTOCK ©

Orlando Farmers Market

Beacham & the Social   LIVE MUSIC

17 ⭐ Map p90, B2

Both the Beacham and the more intimate and recommended Social next door are cornerstones of Orlando's nightclub and live-music scene. They host bands from punk to reggae on the weekends and hop all week long with music and dancing. Shows are designated '18 plus' or '21 plus'. (📞407-246-1419; www.thebeacham.com; 46 N Orange Ave, Downtown; ⊙9pm-3am)

Will's Pub   LIVE MUSIC

18 ⭐ Map p90, E1

With $2 Pabst on tap, pinball and vintage pin-ups on the walls, this is

Orlando's less-polished music scene, but it enjoys a solid reputation as one of the best spots in town to catch local and nationally touring indie music. Smoke-free; beer and wine only. (📞407-898-5070; www.willspub.org; 1042 N Mills Ave, Thornton Park; tickets $8-16; ⊙4pm-2am Mon-Sat, from 6pm Sun)

SAK Comedy Lab   COMEDY

19 ⭐ Map p90, B3

Excellent improv comedy in intimate downtown Orlando theater. It's on the 2nd floor of the City Arts Factory. (📞407-648-0001; www.sakcomedylab.com; 29 S Orange Ave, Downtown; tickets $14, 9pm Tue & Wed $5; ⊙Tue-Sat)

Local Life
Loch Haven Park

Getting There

🚗 Take I-4 Exit 85 (Princeton St) and follow the signs.

🚆 SunRail's Florida Hospital Health Village Station is a 0.2-mile walk from Loch Haven Park.

🚌 Lynx 102, 125

Quiet and picturesque Loch Haven Park, with 45 acres of parkland, giant shade trees and three lakes, clusters some of the city's best museums and theater venues in an oasis of green north of downtown. Wander through the gnarly oaks and dripping cypress, stretch out with a book along the lake, poke through the museums and take in some local theater.

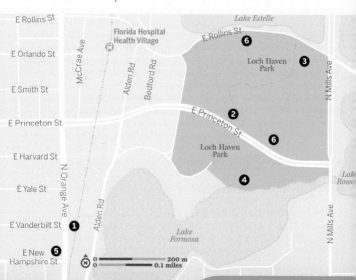

❶ Breakfast at White Wolf

Eclectic and slightly eccentric **White Wolf Cafe** (📞 407-895-9911; www.whitewolf cafe.com; 1829 N Orange Ave, Ivanhoe Village; mains $14-24; ⏱ 8am-3pm Sun-Tue, 8am-9pm Wed & Thu, 8am-10pm Fri & Sat; 🚌 Lynx 102) serves up hearty breakfasts to a hip crowd. A plate of fried chicken with waffles or a stack of fresh raspberry buttermilk pancakes, washed down with a Bloody Mary or two, should keep you fueled for a day at the park.

❷ Hands-On Science

Families and school trips flock to the hands-on displays at **Orlando Science Center** (📞 407-514-2000; www.osc.org; 777 E Princeton St, Loch Haven Park; adult/child $20/14; ⏱ 10am-5pm Thu-Tue; 👶; 🚌 Lynx 125, 🚉 Florida Hospital Health Village). Check out the massive alligators and maybe feed the stingrays; exhibits, with all kinds of interactive displays, are geared to kids aged five to 12, but the natural history 3D movies wow all ages.

❸ Stunning Fine Art

Founded in 1924, the **Orlando Museum of Art** (📞 407-896-4231; www.omart.org; 2416 N Mills Ave, Loch Haven Park; adult/child $15/5; ⏱ 10am-4pm Tue-Fri, from noon Sat & Sun; 👶; 🚌 Lynx 125, 🚉 Florida Hospital Health Village) boasts a small but excellent collection of blown glass, contemporary American graphics, textiles and paintings, and hosts local art events.

❹ Folk Art Museum

Tiny but excellent **Mennello Museum of American Art** (📞 407-246-4278; www. mennellomuseum.org; 900 E Princeton St,

Loch Haven Park, Downtown; adult/child 6-18yr $5/1; ⏱ 10:30am-4:30pm Tue-Sat, from noon Sun; 🚌 Lynx 125, 🚉 Florida Hospital Health Village) features the work of Florida artist Earl Cunningham, whose brightly colored images, a fusion of pop and folk art, leap off the canvas. Changing exhibits include Edward Curtis' American Indian photographs and the Taos Society of Artists.

❺ Craft Beer Garden

With its exposed ceiling pipes, glass mosaic light fixtures and antique furniture, **Imperial Wine Bar & Beer Garden** (📞 407-228-4992; www.imperial winebar.com; 1800 N Orange Ave, Loch Haven Park; snacks $9-16; ⏱ 5pm-midnight Mon-Thu, to 2am Fri & Sat; 🚌 Lynx 102) is a furniture store by day (hence the price tags everywhere) and a neighborhood boho bar by night. Sip on a Cigar City in the quiet nook of a beer garden out back and choose a bite from the limited menu of local fare.

❻ A Night at the Theater

Time your visit to coincide with a show at one of the city's best theater venues. Inside the park, the **John & Rita Lowndes Shakespeare Center** (📞 407-447-1700; www.orlandoshakes.org; 812 E Rollins St, Loch Haven Park; tickets $13-65) hosts everything from Beowulf to The Borrowers, or the **Orlando Repertory Theater** (📞 407-896-7365; www.orlandorep.org; 1001 E Princeton St, Loch Haven Park; tickets $10-25) features performances for families and children exclusively.

Explore

Winter Park

Founded in the mid-19th century and home to the small liberal-arts school Rollins College, bucolic Winter Park concentrates some of Orlando's best-kept secrets – including several of the city's most talked about restaurants and field-to-fork favorites – within a few shaded, pedestrian-friendly streets. Shops, wine bars and sidewalk cafes line Park Ave.

The Sights in a Day

☼ Start off at the **Charles Hosmer Morse Museum of American Art** (p100). You'll want to allow plenty of time to soak in its Tiffany glass and art-nouveau decorative arts.

☼ Stroll along Park Ave, Winter Park's main vein for window shopping, people-watching and wine-sipping. Brand-name stores (Lucky, Lilly Pulitzer, Williams-Sonoma, Restoration Hardware) mix it up with consignment boutiques, spice shops, and boutique pet salons. Pop into any sidewalk cafe for lunch.

☽ After an early farm-to-table dinner at bustling **Prato** (p106) or **Luma on Park** (p107), head to the **Enzian Theater** (p108) for an independent film or cult favorite. Afterwards, while away the night over coffee or a glass of wine at the **Wine Room** (p108).

For a local's day in Winter Park, see p102.

👁 Top Sight

Charles Hosmer Morse Museum of American Art (p100)

◯ Local Life

Fresh & Wild in Winter Park (p102)

♥ Best of Winter Park

Eating
Ethos Vegan Kitchen (p103)

Prato (p106)

Ravenous Pig (p106)

Activities
Scenic Boat Tour (p105)

Getting There

🚗 **Car** From downtown Orlando, take I-4 to Fairbanks Ave and head east for about 2 miles to Park Ave.

🚊 **Rail** Orlando's SunRail (www.sunrail.com) stops at downtown Winter Park.

🚌 **Bus** Lynx 102 services Orange Ave from downtown Orlando to Winter Park.

Top Sights
Charles Hosmer Morse Museum of American Art

Internationally famous, this stunning and delightful museum houses the world's most comprehensive collection of Louis Comfort Tiffany (1848–1933) decorative art. Architectural and art objects salvaged from the artist's Long Island home, including an incredible collection of Favrile pottery, glass work and jewelry, fill multiple galleries.

👁 Map p104, C1

📞 407-645-5311

www.morsemuseum.org

445 N Park Ave

adult/child $6/free

🕘 9:30am-4pm Tue-Sat, from 1pm Sun, to 8pm Fri Nov-Apr

Tiffany Chapel

Laurelton Hall & Daffodil Terrace

Meticulously re-created rooms from Laurelton Hall, Tiffany's 84-room Long Island estate, include massive Tiffany-designed Carrera marble columns topped with glass Daffodil capitals. Photographs, personal letters and selected works tell the story of the artist's life and art.

Lifelines: Forms & Themes of Art Nouveau

More than 100 everyday art objects, including jewelry, vases and tea sets, inspired by nature and organic in style, embody the essence of art nouveau spirit and design. There are more than 50 artists from nine countries on display here – don't miss the peacock feather hand screen, the octopus earthenware vase and the elegant silver lorgnette.

Tiffany Chapel

Featuring 16 glass mosaic-encrusted columns, four leaded glass windows, and furniture of marble and glass, this magnificent chapel was originally designed by Tiffany for the Tiffany Glass and Decorating Company exhibit at the 1893 World's Columbian Exposition in Chicago. In the years after the artist's death, the chapel fell into disrepair and was auctioned off in pieces. The McKeans found and reassembled all the elements, beginning in 1956, and installed the chapel here, in its original form.

Secrets of Tiffany Glassmaking

While most of us are familiar with the look of the iconic Tiffany-glass lamps, the how-to behind the art remains a bit of a mystery to the layman. Several galleries explain the science and production processes behind Tiffany's ground-breaking glasswork and offer a history of his studio.

☑ Top Tips

▶ From November through April, admission is free on Friday from 4pm to 8pm.

▶ Free parking is available along Park Ave, directly behind the museum and on the 1st, 4th and 5th floors of the Park Place garage on Canton Ave.

▶ The museum offers first-come first-serve tours of Laurelton Hall at 11am and 2:30pm Tuesday and Thursday.

✗ Take a Break

Fuel up with a breakfast of cheese grits and fried green tomatoes at Briarpatch (p108), a couple of blocks down the street from the museum, or swing by for a slice of mile-high cake. For a post-museum drink, the Wine Room (p108) offers more than 150 wines in 1oz, 2.5oz or 5oz pours.

Local Life
Fresh & Wild in Winter Park

A fresh and wild day in this dog-friendly college town is a perfect antidote to the crowds and high-octane fun of Orlando theme parks' sensory overload. Amble through Winter Park's gardens and historic districts, linger for coffee at a sidewalk cafe and enjoy the evening over wine and farm-to-table cuisine.

❶ Pastries at Croissant Gourmet

Befitting Winter Park's European vibe, start the day with coffee and a pastry at the tiny Paris-perfect **Croissant Gourmet** (📞407-622-7753; www.facebook.com/thecroissantgourmet; 120 E Morse Blvd; mains $8-12; ⏰7am-6pm Sun-Thu, to 8pm Fri & Sat; kitchen closes 6pm daily). There are classic éclairs, delicious blueberry tarts and massive cinnamon twists, as

well as sweet and savory crepes, traditional French breakfasts and lunches, and wine by the glass.

❷ Boating Through the Neighborhood

One of the best ways to appreciate Winter Park is by cruising on a one-hour Scenic Boat Tour (p105) on Lake Osceola.

❸ Vegan Delights

Take a break from the hearty, meaty and seafood portions, favored by the farm-to-table crowd. **Ethos Vegan Kitchen** (📞407-228-3898; www.ethosvegankitchen.com; 601b S New York Ave; mains $7-14; ⊙11am-11pm Mon-Fri; 🖋) offers a range of delights such as pizza with broccoli, banana peppers, zucchini and seitan; pecan-encrusted eggplant; homemade soups and various sandwiches with names such as A Fungus Among Us and Hippie Wrap.

❹ Lingering Over Wine & Art

Head to **Alfond Inn** (📞407-998-8090; www.thealfondinn.com; 300 E New England Ave; r from $309; ❄@🛜≋🐾) for a coffee or a wine, followed by a curated tour of their extraordinary modern

art collection, part of the Cornell Fine Arts Museum, which is exhibited here. If this portion has intrigued you, pop over to the museum (p105) for the rest of the collection.

❺ Lakeside Sculpture Garden

Listed on the National Register of Historic Places and perched on the shore of Lake Osceola, the **Albin Polasek Museum & Sculpture Gardens** (www.polasek.org; 633 Osceola Ave; adult/child $5/free; ⊙10am-4pm Tue-Sat, from 1pm Sun) was home to Czech sculptor Albin Polasek. His small yellow villa serves as a museum of his life and work, and the lovely lakeside gardens house some of his organically fluid bronzes.

❻ Locally Sourced Feast

Head to the Ravenous Pig (p106) for a pre-dinner tipple in its fabulous on-site brewery. Then sit down within the same industrial chic premises, for a gourmet feast. Describing the meals sounds like a page out of a foodie review using the phrases 'foodie's farm-to-table, sustainable, creative extravaganza'. Err, cough. Forgive us: that's exactly what it is. Reserve ahead.

Charles Hosmer Morse
Museum of American Art

WINTER PARK

Scenic
Boat Tour 1

For reviews see

	Top Sights	p100
	Sights	p105
	Eating	p106
	Drinking	p108
	Entertainment	p108
	Shopping	p109

400 m
0.2 miles

Lake
Osceola

Lake
Virginia

Dinky Dock
Park

Cornell
Fine Arts
Museum 2

Osceola Ct

Osceola Ave

Chase Ave

Chase Ave

E New England Ave

E New England Ave

S Interlachen Ave

Holt Ave

E Fairbanks Ave

Fairbanks Ave

E Lyman Ave

S Park Ave

E Welborne Ave

E Morse Blvd

Lincoln Ave

N Knowles Ave

N Center St

E Canton Ave

Cole Ave

W Swoope Ave

N Interlachen Ave

18

19 20

8 14

5 7

16

13

11

Breakaway Bikes

Central
Park

Winter
Park

W Park Ave

S New York Ave

N New York Ave

W New York Ave

W Canton Ave

Garfield Ave

Carolina Ave

N Virginia Ave

Symonds Ave

S Capen Ave

Douglas Ave

15

10

W Morse Blvd

W New England Ave

W Welborne Ave

W Lyman Ave

Shady
Park

Hannibal
Square
Heritage
Center

3

9

17

S Pennsylvania Ave

S Virginia Ave

6

S Comstock Ave

W Fairbanks Ave

W Comstock Ave

S Fairbanks Ave

S Orange Ave

Holt Ave

12

4

Cornell Fine Arts Museum

Sights

Scenic Boat Tour BOATING

1 ⊙ Map p104, D2

One of the best ways to appreciate the under-the-radar beauty and classic Florida escape of Winter Park is to meander over to Lake Osceola for a one-hour boat tour. You learn much about the area's history and gossip about the houses on the lake. Hop on an 18-passenger pontoon and cruise through Winter Park's tropical canals and lakes, past mansions, Rollins College and other sites. They also rent canoes and rowboats (☎407-644-4056; www.scenicboattours.com; 312 E Morse Blvd; adult/child $14/7; ⊙hourly 10am-4pm; 👪)

Cornell Fine Arts Museum MUSEUM

2 ⊙ Map p104, E4

This tiny lakeside museum on the campus of Rollins College houses an eclectic collection of historic and contemporary US, European and Latin American art. (www.rollins.edu/cfam; Rollins College, 1000 Holt Ave; admission free; ⊙10am-7pm Tue, 10am-4pm Wed-Fri, noon-5pm Sat & Sun)

Hannibal Square Heritage Center MUSEUM

3 ⊙ Map p104, A3

As far back as 1881, Winter Park's Hannibal Square was home to African Americans employed as carpenters, farmers and household help. The *Heritage Collection: Photographs and Oral Histories of West Winter Park 1900–1980,* on permanent display at this little museum, celebrates and preserves this community's culture and history. (☎407-539-2860; www.hannibalsquareheritagecenter.org; 642 W New England Ave; admission free; ◷noon-4pm Tue-Thu, to 5pm Fri, 10am-2pm Sat)

Kraft Azalea Gardens   PARK

4 ◉ Map p104, D1

Quiet lakeside park with enormous cypress trees. Particularly stunning January through March, when the azaleas burst into bloom. There's a dock, but no barbecues or picnic tables. (https://cityofwinterpark.org/departments/parks-recreation/parks-playgrounds/parks/kraft-azalea-garden; 1365 Alabama Dr; ◷8am-dusk)

Breakaway Bikes   CYCLING

5 ◉ Map p104, C2

Rent a bike from Breakaway Bikes and ask for their Scenic Bike Ride map. The 4-mile pedal takes you up to quiet lakeside Kraft Azalea Gardens (p106), with its huge cypress trees and blooming azaleas (January through

Top Tip

Sidewalk Art Festival

One of the oldest art festivals in the country where more than 220 artists display work along the sidewalks of small-town Winter Park.

March), past historic neighborhoods, and through the lovely campus of **Rollins College**. Pause at **Dinky Dock Park** to dangle your feet in the waters of Lake Virginia and watch the students paddleboard. (☎407-622-2453; www.breakawaybicycleswinterpark.com; 141 Lincoln Ave; per hour/day $10/35; ◷10am-6pm Tue-Sat, 11am-5pm Sun)

Eating

Ravenous Pig   AMERICAN $$$

6 ✕ Map p104, B4

The cornerstone of Orlando's restaurant trend for locally sourced food, this chef-owned hipster spot moved to its new location in 2016. Here it's all about letting the food do the talking: locavore, omnivore, carnivore – take your pick. Really ravenous pigs can get their teeth into the pork porterhouse or the local seafood (the shrimp and grits is a must; $15). Don't miss. (☎407-628-2333; www.theravenouspig.com; 565 W Fairbanks; mains $14-32; ◷11:30am-3pm & 5-10pm Mon-Sat, 10:30am-3pm & 5-9pm Sun)

Prato   ITALIAN $$$

7 ✕ Map p104, C2

A hopping go-to spot with high ceilings, exposed beams and a bar expanding the length of the room. Offers inspired interpretations of classic Italian dishes, house-cured meats and excellent wood-oven pizza ($16). (☎407-262-0050; www.prato-wp.com; 124 N Park Ave; mains $16-33; ◷11:30am-4:30pm Mon & Tues, to 11pm Wed-Sat, to 10pm Sun)

Luma on Park

AMERICAN $$$

8 Map p104, C3

A must for upscale foodie delights, not to mention people-watching. The menu features rather complicated pairings such as 'red snapper with black and white quinoa, braised watermelon radish, English pea, delta asparagus and citrus olive tapenade.' The recommended $35 prix-fixe menu is offered Sunday, Monday and Tuesday only. (☏407-599-4111; www. lumaonpark.com; 290 S Park Ave; mains $25-30; ☺5:30-10pm Mon-Thu, 5.30-11pm Fri & Sat, 5.30-9pm Sun)

Dexter's of Winter Park

AMERICAN $$

9 Map p104, B3

Unpretentious Winter Park go-to spot for creative American fare off the beaten track of Park Ave. There's live music Wednesday through Sunday, primarily of the funk, soul, jazz and blues variety, sidewalk seating and a popular Sunday brunch. Try the pressed duck sandwich, with grilled onions and melted brie ($15). (☏407-629-1150; www. dexwine.com; 558 W New England Ave; mains $10-26; ☺11am-10pm Mon-Thu, to midnight Fri & Sat, 10am-10pm Sun)

The Coop

SOUTHERN US $

10 Map p104, B2

Line up for massive plates of smothered pork chops, fried chicken or chicken potpie, with sides of fried okra, creamed corn, maple-glazed

Winter Park Farmers Market (p108)

carrots and other Southern classics. Cafeteria-style, with 'make-a-friend' tables or call ahead for sidewalk pick-up. (☏407-843-2667; www.asouthernaffair .com; 610 W Morse Blvd; mains $10-14; ☺7am-8pm Mon-Thu, to 9pm Fri & Sat)

Orchid Thai Cuisine

THAI $

11 Map p104, C2

Contemporary and tasty with pleasant pavement seating. Don't miss the delectable 'Thai Doughnuts': dough balls fried with a sweet condensed-milk dressing and sprinkled with crushed peanuts. (☏407-331-1400; www.orchidthai winterpark.com; 305 N Park Ave; mains $8-15;

Local Life

Winter Park Farmers Market

Winter Park's historic train station, with its original brick walls and massive vintage wooden sliding doors, houses the Saturday-morning Winter Park Farmers Market. You'll find local cheeses and honey, flowers and herbs, along with several excellent stands selling baked goods, spread out in the station and through the gardens.

⏱11am-9pm Mon-Wed, 11am-10pm Thu-Sat, noon-9pm Sun; 🛫)

4 Rivers Smokehouse   BARBECUE $

12 ✕ Map p104, A4

Expect lines out the door at this regular (chain) contender for best barbecue in Orlando. (☎407-474-8377; https://4rsmokehouse.com; 1600 W Fairbanks Ave; mains $8-18; ⏱11am-8pm Mon-Thu, to 9pm Fri & Sat)

Briarpatch   CAFE $$

13 ✕ Map p104, C2

Massive multilayer cakes and hearty breakfasts in white-washed, shabby-chic tearoom environs. A locals' fave for brunches. (☎407-628-8651; 252 N Park Ave; mains $8-18; ⏱7am-5pm Mon-Fri, 8am-5pm Sat & Sun; 👪)

Drinking

Wine Room   WINE BAR

14 Map p104, C3

It's a bit of a gimmick, but you purchase a wine card and put as much money on it as you'd like. Then simply slide your card into the automated servers for whichever wine looks good, press the button for a taste or a full glass, and enjoy. More than 150 wines, arranged by region and type. (☎407-696-9463; www.thewineroomonline.com; 270 S Park Ave; tastings from $2.50; ⏱2pm-midnight Mon-Wed, from noon Thu, 11:30am-1:30am Fri & Sat, noon-11pm Sun)

Entertainment

Enzian Theater   CINEMA

15 ⭐ Map p104, A2

The envy of any college town, this clapboard-sided theater screens independent and classic films, and has the excellent **Eden Bar** (☎407-629-1088; ⏱11am-11pm Sun-Thu, to 1am Fri & Sat; 🛫) restaurant, featuring primarily local and organic fare. Have a veggie burger and a beer on the patio underneath the cypress tree or opt for table service in the theater. (☎407-629-0054; www.enzian.org; 1300 S Orlando Ave, Maitland; adult/child $10/8; ⏱5pm-midnight Tue-Fri, noon-midnight Sat & Sun)

Popcorn Flicks in the Park
CINEMA

16 ⭐ Map p104, C2

Bring a picnic and a blanket, and kick back under the stars for a free outdoor film classic. (☎407-629-1088; www.enzian. org; 251 S Park Ave, Central Park; ⊘8pm 2nd Thu of the month; 🚼)

Shopping

Rifle Paper Co
STATIONERY

17 🔒 Map p104, B3

This tiny retail space, started by a husband and wife team in 2009, sells lovely paper stationery products. It now also ships internationally. (☎407-622-7679; www.riflepaperco.com; 558 W New England Ave; ⊘9am-6pm Mon-Fri, 10am-5pm Sat)

Rocket Fizz
FOOD

18 🔒 Map p104, C4

Satisfy any kind of sweet tooth in this candy emporium, with 1200 different kinds of candy from countries around the world, several hundred varieties of glass-bottled soda and all kinds of gag gifts. Sure, there's classic chocolate and buckets of saltwater taffy, but how about that bacon frosting you always wanted to try? Or french-fry lip balm and candy cigarettes? (☎407-645-3499; www.rocketfizz.com; 520 S Park Ave; ⊘10:30am-9pm Mon-Thu, 11am-11pm Fri & Sat, 11am-8pm Sun)

Lighten Up Toy Store
TOYS

19 🔒 Map p104, C3

Small but well-stocked toy store with classics such as marbles and kazoos, outdoor toys including Frisbees, boomerangs and kites, and restaurant-perfect activity and picture books. There's an entire wall of games and puzzles and, for those rainy days stuck in the hotel, 'furniture-friendly bow and arrow rockets.' (☎407-644-3528; 348 S Park Ave; ⊘10am-5pm Mon-Sat)

Peterbrooke Chocolatier of Winter Park
CHOCOLATE

20 🔒 Map p104, C3

High-end chocolate boutique with decadent house-made concoctions and exotic-flavored gelati. Try the bourbon caramel ginger. (☎407-644-3200; 300 S Park Ave; ⊘10am-10pm Mon-Thu, 10am-11pm Fri & Sat, 11am-10pm Sun)

Top Sights
Kennedy Space Center

Getting There

🚌 Gray Line offers round-trip transportation from Orlando locations ($59).

🚗 The Space Center is east across the NASA Pkwy on SR 405. Parking costs $10.

One of Florida's most visited attractions, this 140,000-acre site was once the US' primary space-flight facility, where shuttles were built and astronauts rocketed into the cosmos. Although NASA indefinitely terminated its shuttle program in 2011, shifting the center from a living museum to a historical one, new plans are afoot to send astronauts to the moon, Mars and beyond.

For a schedule of crewless rocket and satellite launches, visit www.spacecoastlaunches.com. Time your visit to coincide with one of these.

Apollo/Saturn V Center

Kennedy Space Center Bus Tour

This 90-minute tour is the only way to see beyond the Visitor Complex without paying for an add-on tour. The bus winds through the launch facilities to the **Apollo/Saturn V Center**, where you can see the 363ft, 6.5-million-lb *Saturn V* moon rocket and catch a multimedia show depicting America's first lunar mission.

Space Shuttle Atlantis

Blasted by rocket fuel and streaked with space dust, space shuttle *Atlantis*, the final orbiter among NASA's fleet, is suspended in a specially designed display. Interactive consoles invite visitors to try to land it or dock it to the International Space Station and a short film tells the story of the shuttle program from its inception in the 1960s to *Atlantis'* final mission in 2011.

Heroes & Legends and the U.S. Astronaut Hall of Fame

The center's newest exhibit celebrates pioneers of NASA's early space programs, inspiring a new generation to keep their intergalactic dreams alive. It starts with a 360-degree film on the lives of astronauts, then guides visitors through displays of a Redstone rocket, space shuttles and astronauts' personal belongings. The exhibit also features the Mercury Mission Control room and the 4D movie *Through the Eyes of a Hero*, about the lives of the 93 Hall of Fame inductees.

Rocket Garden

Wander among real and replica rocket capsules that launched the American Space Program. You can climb into some of them – it's amazing to see how tiny the cockpits are, and to imagine real astronauts sitting exactly where are you are sitting. But instead of sipping on that giant Dr Pepper in the Florida sun, they were shooting up through

☑ 866-737-5235

www.kennedyspace
center.com

NASA Pkwy, Merritt
Island

adult/child 3-11yr $50/40

⊙9am-6pm

☑ Top Tips

▶ The three add-on tours must be reserved in advance; multiple add-ons require more than a one-day visit.

▶ All attractions are wheelchair accessible, and complimentary strollers and wheelchairs are provided.

✗ Take a Break

Seafood lovers swoon over the freshly caught sustainable goodies at **Wild Ocean Seafood** (www.wildoceanmarket.com; 688 S Park Ave; mains $9-12; ⊙11am-6pm Mon-Thu, 10am-6pm Fri & Sat, 11am-4pm Sun) market. Head across the causeway, seven miles north on Hwy 1 and west on South St.

Understand

Space Missions Then & Now

Early Space Exploration

In 1949 President Harry S Truman established the Joint Long Range Proving Grounds at Cape Canaveral for missile testing. The first rocket was launched on July 24, 1950, and in 1958 the National Aeronautics and Space Administration (NASA) was born to 'carry out the peaceful exploration and use of space.'

Though Soviet cosmonaut Yuri Gagarin took the honor of the first man in space on April 12, 1961, Alan Shepard became the first American one month later. In February 1962 John Glenn launched from Cape Canaveral, circled the Earth three times in the world's first orbital flight, and landed four hours later in the Atlantic Ocean off Bermuda.

Project Apollo & Space Shuttle Program

John Glenn's seminal voyage fueled support for the space program, and President Kennedy vowed to land a man on the moon by the end of the decade. On July 16, 1969, a *Saturn V* rocket shot out from Kennedy Space Center. Four days later Neil Armstrong spoke the immortal phrase: 'That's one small step for man, one giant leap for mankind.' Between 1969 and 1972, six more Apollo missions launched to explore the moon.

In 1976 NASA introduced the space shuttle, a reusable manned space vehicle designed to rocket into space with a booster (which is later shed), orbit the earth, and glide back safely to solid ground. Five years later, in 1981, NASA's successful launch of the *STS-1*, piloted by John Young and Robert Crippen, opened a new era of American space exploration. Tragedy struck, however, with the January 28, 1986 *Challenger* explosion. Seven astronauts were killed, including schoolteacher Christa McAuliffe, who was to be the first ordinary citizen to go into space. NASA stopped all launches until that of shuttle *Discovery* in 1988. Throughout the 1990s, shuttles allowed American astronauts to maintain the Hubble Space Telescope and help construct the International Space Station.

On February 1, 2003, *Columbia* exploded upon reentry, again killing all seven astronauts on board, and NASA again stopped the shuttle program. Missions resumed in 2005, but closed indefinitely in 2011.

Understand
Meet an Astronaut

There are two ways to meet an astronaut at Kennedy Space Center. The first is at the **Astronaut Encounter**, held daily inside the Astronaut Encounter Theater and included in park admission. Don't confuse this with the Mission Status Briefing, held in the same theater, which offers lectures on the past, present and future of space exploration but does not feature a real live astronaut. Check your park map for times.

The second is **Lunch with an Astronaut** (adult/child $30/16), in which an astronaut presents a short talk on his or her experiences while guests eat, and then opens the floor for questions. Register in advance online, or check same-day availability at the Ticket Plaza upon entering the park.

the atmosphere. Little ones can cool off in the spurting fountain on the far corner of Rocket Garden.

Space Mirror Memorial

The stunningly beautiful Space Mirror Memorial, a shiny granite wall standing four stories high, reflects both literally and figuratively the personal and tragic stories behind the theme-park energy that permeates the center. Several stone panels display the photos and names of those who died in space disasters.

IMAX Theater

Within the Visitor Complex, an IMAX theater shows two delightful films that include clear explanations of complicated science and footage shot from space. *A Beautiful Planet* offers a look at the effect of humans on planet earth and an optimistic take on the future, narrated by Jennifer Lawrence, and *Journey to Space 3D* features interviews with astronauts and an exciting overview of NASA's past, present and future undertakings.

Add-on Experiences

Extended tours offer the opportunity to visit the **Vehicle Assembly Building**, **Cape Canaveral Air Force Station** and its launch sites and the **Launch Control Center**, where engineers perform system checks. Great for kids, **Lunch with an Astronaut** offers a chance to hang out with a real astronaut, while the **Cosmic Quest** is an action-oriented game-play experience featuring real NASA missions involving rocket launch, redirection of an asteroid and building a Martian habitat.

Top Sights
Legoland® Florida Resort

Getting There

🚌 The Legoland Shuttle ($5) runs daily from I-Drive 360 (near the Orlando Eye).

🚗 Park on the bottom floor of the I-Drive 360 parking lot (free).

Legoland is a joy. It feels different to Orlando's other theme parks. There's no in-your-face special effects, no elaborate parades or shows, no blaring music. Sure, lines can get long, but crowds pale in comparison to the big hitters and you don't have to plan like a general to enjoy a strikingly stress-free and relaxed day. Rides and attractions, including the attached water park, are geared towards children ages two to 12. It is a superb way of making play educational and fun.

The Dragon

Rides & Shows

There's plenty for little ones to love, including a foam ball play area, splash fountains and kiddie rides. At **Ford Driving School**, tiny tots can drive cars through a pretend town and earn an official license, and the lakeside water-ski show is pure silly pirate fun. The park's roller coaster thrills are **Project x**, **The Dragon**, **Coastersaurus** (the park's classic wooden coaster), plus **Flying School**, a coaster that zips you around with your feet dangling free; the water park offers high-speed slides and a lazy river. Kids love **Mia's Riding Adventure**, a horse-themed 'disc' coaster.

Miniland USA

Anyone who has ever tried to build with Lego bricks will be wowed by the intricate designs and painstaking detail of these Lego models of iconic American cities as well as scenes from *Star Wars* films. Though amazingly accurate, there's a sense of humor here, such as the interactive water and sound features. Oh, and keep an eye out for whimsical scenarios such as the crazy cat lady.

Ninjago

Ninjago is Legoland's new martial art–themed area. As well as meeting characters, including Kai, this section includes an interactive ride where you can score points using different ninja hand maneuvers to zap fireballs, lightning and the like. As seen through your 4D glasses, of course. It's remarkable technology and such fun.

Imagination Zone

Don't miss this wonderful indoor space. It's a great stop during or after having looked at the park's works of Lego 'art.' This colorful, interactive learning center has themed zones and skilled Lego makers are on hand to help children of all ages create something from the thousands of Lego bricks.

☏863-318-5346

http://florida.legoland.com

1 Legoland Way

1-/2-day tickets adult $93/113, 3-12yr $86/106

⊙10am-5pm

🚌Legoland Shuttle

☑ Top Tips

▶ Buying entry tickets at least two days ahead will save you cash.

▶ If you're with little 'uns under two years old, take advantage of the 'tot spots' with Duplo among other things (while older siblings enjoy the rides elsewhere).

✕ Take a Break

Stop by the retro-dive **Donut Man** (☏863-293-4031; 1290 6th St; donuts from $1; ⊙5am-10pm; ♿) for donuts on the way to Legoland. For lunch in the park, pick up a sandwich from Lakeside Sandwich Co, and relax by the giant Banyan tree in Cypress Gardens.

The Best of

Orlando & Walt Disney World® Resort

The Simpsons Ride (p61), Universal Studios
MIAMI2YOU/SHUTTERSTOCK ©

Best
For Under Fives

MIAM2YOU/SHUTTERSTOCK ©

Families with little ones, loaded down with strollers, car-seats and soft-sided cooler packs, flock to Orlando by the hundreds of thousands every year. The main draw, of course, is the theme parks, and the challenge for parents is digging through the overwhelming options and inflated rhetoric to find what best suits your time, budget and family.

Theme Parks

Ride-through-stories, gentle spins on fanciful creatures and brightly colored splash play areas entertain little ones for hours and days. Children three years and younger don't pay theme-park admission. At Walt Disney World® Resort, Universal Orlando Resort and SeaWorld, baby care centers provide quiet places for nursing and downtime, sell diapers, over-the-counter children's medication and more; some also offer a full kitchen. Look for them on park maps.

Downtime

A vacation to Central Florida and the theme parks can be exhausting for children and adults alike, and you'd be surprised at how difficult it can be to carve out downtime. Orlando hotels have lazy rivers, toddler-friendly slides and zero-entry pools, beaches and playgrounds. An occasional lazy morning, lunch reservations in an air-conditioned restaurant, and long afternoons at the hotel pool do wonders for everyone's spirits.

☑ **Top Tip**

▶ Little ones too young for Harry Potter and the Forbidden Journey can simply walk through Hogwarts magical charms – the separate line for this isn't marked, so just ask.

Best For Rides

Seuss Landing Charmingly whimsical Seuss-themed rides, play area and story performance. (p66)

Fantasyland Toddler-perfect storybook rides, 3D Donald Duck movie and princesses everywhere. (p25)

Legoland Smaller, less crowded and rides without any trace of scary special effects. (p114)

Seuss Landing (p66), Islands of Adventure

Best Shows

Finding Nemo: The Musical Magnificent puppets transform *Finding Nemo* into a Broadway-style musical. (p35)

Beauty and the Beast – Live on Stage Belle, the Beast and a magical rose

beautifully staged in an outdoor theater. (p39)

Festival of the Lion King Interactive singing and dancing performance. (p36)

Voyage of the Little Mermaid Back-lit stage

show with bubbles and Disney crooning. (p41)

Best for Water Play

Typhoon Lagoon Beautiful surrounds with plenty for all ages. (p46)

Worth a Trip

Only 30 minutes' drive southeast from Disney, **Green Meadows Farm** (☎407-846-0770; www.greenmeadowsfarm.com; 1368 S Poinciana Blvd, Kissimee; adult/3-12yr $23/20; ⏱9:30am-4:30pm, final tour 2:30pm) makes a pleasant countryside getaway. Several tours daily take you to pet the animals, milk a cow, ride a pony and more. There's also plenty of shade and grass, a picnic area and a playground.

Best
For Five- to 12-Year Olds

While Orlando offers something for all ages, it offers just about everything for this age group. They're young enough to marvel wide-eyed with faith that dreams really do come true, to giggle with delight at a hug from Snow White and stand awed by magical happenings, but they're also old enough for most of the rides. Some families, in fact, return year after sunburned year.

Florida's Wilder Side

Even if you're coming for Orlando's theme parks, consider taking some time away from their spinning wheels of eye candy to explore the parks and lakes in and around the city. You don't have to be a hard-core outdoor enthusiast or go very far to take a peek into Florida's wilder side, which makes it perfect for kids – within an hour of Walt Disney World®, you can be paddling calm waters past alligators, turtles and heron, or tubing down a spring-fed river.

Eating & Drinking

Sure, you'll find chicken nuggets and burgers, lemonade and cola in all the parks, but the real fun is whimsical theming of the parks' food and drink. The Flaming Moe in Universal Studio's Springville bubbles with smoke, tiny 'fish eggs' settle on the bottom of Diagon Alley's Fishy Green Ale, and Seuss' fruity Moose Juice comes fresh or frozen. And at Disney, even the butter on your breakfast tray comes stamped with Mickey Mouse.

Best Coasters

Big Thunder Mountain Railroad Gentle coaster through the Wild West. (p27)

Flight of the Hippogriff Listen for Fang's barks and don't forget to bow to Buckbeak. (p67)

Dragon Challenge Gut-churning dueling roller coasters. (p67)

Expedition Everest Zip backwards to escape the Yeti. (p35)

Best Classics

Peter Pan's Flight Gentle flight through the story and over London. (p25)

Mad Tea Party Quintessential Disney spinning. (p43)

Festival of Fantasy Daytime parade with current

Jurassic Park River Adventure (p65), Islands of Adventure

favorites from animations and more. (p28)

Pirates of the Caribbean Slow cruise through the world of pirates. (p27)

Mickey's PhilharMagic A 3D jaunt into classic Disney movies. (p25)

Make a Splash

Splash Mountain Animatronic animals and a classic watery splash. (p26)

Popeye & Bluto's Bilge-Rat Barges White-water rafting guaranteed to get you soaked. (p66)

Dudley Do-Right's Ripsaw Falls Water ride silliness with a 75ft plunge. (p66)

Jurassic Park River Adventure Dinosaur themed. (p65)

Volcano Bay Water park modeled on a Pacific island, with watery thrills and spills running through a giant volcano. (p69)

Best TV- & Movie-Based Rides

Harry Potter and the Forbidden Journey Wind through the Hogwarts and fly over the school in a quidditch match. (p65)

Star Tours Take a virtual reality tour through the galaxy with Chewbacca and Han Solo. (p39)

Despicable Me: Minion Mayhem Minions, minions and more minions in marvelous 3D simulation. (p62)

Toy Story Midway Mania! Ride-through video game. (p41)

Best Educational

Titanic the Experience Board the Titanic, with characters in period dress and re-created rooms. (p81)

Orlando Science Center See 3D movies and interactive science. (p97)

Best
For Teenagers

Edgy rides and thrills, high-speed waterslides, TV- and movie-themed everything, eat-in multiplex cinemas and video arcades with some of the best game technology in the country – what more could a teenager want? And at Walt Disney World® Resort and Universal Orlando Resort, everything is connected by boat, bus or monorail, so teenagers can easily head out to explore on their own.

CRAIG RUSSELL/SHUTTERSTOCK ©

Universal vs Disney

Teenagers love Universal Orlando Resort. Not only does it promise some of Orlando's biggest thrills, but it does everything just a bit smarter, a bit funnier and a bit more smoothly than Disney. Instead of the Seven Dwarfs, there's the Simpsons. Instead of Donald Duck and Mickey Mouse, there's Spider-Man and Shrek. Universal certainly lacks the sentimental charm of Cinderella, Peter Pan and Winnie-the-Pooh, but it's got spunk, it's got attitude.

Exploring on Their Own

The self-contained worlds of Walt Disney World® Resort and especially the smaller Universal Orlando Resort are uniquely amenable to older teens heading out to explore on their own. They don't need to drive or take a cab to get around, as everything is connected by boat, bus or monorail; it's easy to find your way (and if you do get lost or confused there's staff everywhere); and the rides and attractions will keep them happy for hours and days.

☑ **Top Tips**

▶ Epcot's Soarin' is arguably Disney's best attraction for cross-generational guests. Reserve with FastPass+ or hit it when the gates open.

▶ Escape from Gringotts and Harry Potter and the Forbidden Journey are two of the few rides at Universal Orlando Resort that don't offer ExpressPass lines. Waits can reach beyond hours; visit them first thing.

Outdoor Activities

While Orlando's primary draw for teens is of course the theme parks, consider carving out time to dip into Florida's wild side. There's excellent novice-friendly canoeing, tubing, kayaking and hiking just outside the city, and the beaches of Canaveral National Seashore are just over an hour's drive away.

MARK & AUDREY GIBSON/AGE FOTOSTOCK ©

Typhoon Lagoon (p46)

Best Simulated Rides

Escape from Gringotts You, along with Harry and his friends, are mistaken as an intruder into 'the safest place on earth.' (p61)

The Simpsons Ride A trip to Krusty the Clown's amusement park turns wild when crazy Sideshow Bob seeks revenge on the Simpsons. (p61)

Revenge of the Mummy Indoor multisensory coaster. (p62)

Best for Rainy Days

Imagination Zone A wonderfully fun and educative zone within Legoland, with helpers at hand. (p115)

WonderWorks A 36ft indoor ropes course, a 4D theater with changing shows, laser tag and all kinds of frenetic interactive exhibits. (p81)

I Fly Orlando Indoor skydiving in a controlled environment. (p82)

Best Water Parks

Typhoon Lagoon Beautiful surrounds, massive wave pool with 6ft swells, and surfing lessons. (p46)

Blizzard Beach Brace yourself for some seriously high-octane thrills and heart-stopping speeds. (p46)

Best for Nighttime

CityWalk Live music, a cineplex movie theater

and teen nights at the Groove. (p76)

Hollywood Drive-In Golf LED-lit, sci-fi or haunted house–themed miniature-golf. (p70)

Blue Man Group Over-the-top silliness and audience interaction. (p77)

Best Dining

Sci-Fi Dine-In Theater Milkshakes and burgers in a mock drive-in theater. (p39)

'Ohana Giant skewers of beef and chicken served family-style. (p50)

Hamburger Mary's Burger joint with raucous interactive Sunday brunch. (p93)

Best
For Adults

Orlando may tout itself as a family destination but there are abundant opportunities for adults to enjoy themselves in the Theme Park Capital of the World.

MIAMI2YOU/SHUTTERSTOCK ©

Best Tours

Keys to the Kingdom
Popular five-hour tour into the Magic Kingdom's secrets (no children allowed). (p145)

Best for Romance

Luma on Park Dark surrounds and elegant fare. (p107)

Victoria & Albert's The only place in Disney that doesn't allow kids. (p51)

Narcoossee's A lovely boat from Magic Kingdom to waterfront peace and quiet. (p52)

California Grill Rooftop grill with firework views. (p48)

Best for Drinking

World Showcase Eat and drink around the world in marvelously themed surrounds. (p32)

Wine Room A serve-yourself wine bar with sidewalk seating and tasty fare. (p108)

CityWalk Dance clubs, live music and outdoor drinking. (p76)

Best for Laughs

Islands of Adventure Splashing, zipping and 3D wows. (p64)

Universal Studios Home to The Simpson Ride and some of Orlando's biggest thrills. (p60)

Hamburger Mary's Drag shows, Broadway tunes and excellent burgers. (p93)

Best Local Entertainment

Enzian Theater Indie favorites and a tiki bar. (p108)

Tanqueray's Unassuming downstairs bar with local live music. (p94)

Top Tips

▶ Both Disney and Universal offer childcare centers, and recommend babysitting services for in-room sitting and extra help at the theme parks.

▶ Both Universal's CityWalk and Downtown Disney offer dine-in multiplex theaters. Call ☎407-354-3374 for showtimes at Universal and ☎407-827-1308 for showtimes at Disney.

▶ For a neighborhood vibe with sidewalk cafes, wine bars and pedestrian-friendly wanderings, head to Winter Park or Thornton Park, east of Lake Eola.

Best
Theme Park Thrills

As the Theme Park Capital of the World, Orlando offers plenty of knuckle-biting, stomach-sinking, screaming thrills. But the thrills here go beyond the usual zipping coaster variety – special effects, 3D glasses and narrative twists give most of the city's thrill rides that distinct Orlando-centric style.

MIAMI2YOU/SHUTTERSTOCK ©

Incredible Hulk Coaster Screams from this crown-jewel, filled with corkscrews, loops and dips, echo through Islands of Adventure. (p65)

Harry Potter and the Forbidden Journey Soar through Hogwarts and past Dementors with Harry, Hermione and Fred. (p65)

Dragon Challenge Twist, turn and loop, feet dangling free on one of two intertwined coasters, the Chinese Fireball or the Hungarian Horntail – a Hogsmeade favorite. (p65)

Hollywood Rip Ride Rockit Arguably the most terrifying (um, thrilling) coaster in Orlando – choose your own music and prepare to loop and plummet at Universal Studios. (p62)

Revenge of the Mummy This Universal Studios coaster combines serious speed and twists with in-your-face special effects. (p62)

Twilight Zone Tower of Terror An elevator takes you clatter, clatter, clatter, up into a haunted hotel, and free falls down. (p38)

Harry Potter and the Escape from Gringotts Universal Studio's hottest ride takes you from Diagon Alley into Gringotts Bank, past the bank-teller goblins, and into a 3D multisensory Harry Potter world. (p61)

Space Mountain This indoor Magic Kingdom classic zips into star-

☑ **Top Tips**

▶ Universal Orlando Resort and Legoland offer add-on tickets that give front-of-the-line or special express-line access for select attractions. Guests at Universal Orlando Resort's deluxe hotels receive a complimentary unlimited Express Pass.

▶ Wait times in single-rider lines can be a sliver of what they are in regular lines. If a single-rider line is not clearly marked, ask an attendant.

studded galaxies of outer space, but it has no terrifying dips or loops. (p28)

Best
Interactive Experiences

Rides, shows and restaurants, both in and out of the theme park, offer dozens of opportunities to interact with TV and movie characters. The basic concept behind most of the theme parks' simulated rides is that you yourself are a character in the movie or TV show, and the movie characters talk directly to you – in Minion Mayhem, for example, the premise is that Gru is recruiting you to be a minion.

CRAIG RUSSELL/SHUTTERSTOCK ©

☑ **Top Tips**

▶ For a list of which Disney characters can be found where, go to www.disneyworld.disney.go.com and scroll down 'Things to Do' to 'Character Experiences.' Make reservations online, at My Disney Experience or on ☎407-939-3463.

▶ See Kenny the Pirate (http://kennythepirate.com) for everything you need to know about meeting Disney characters.

▶ See p150 for more on Disney character experiences.

Character Meals

Both Walt Disney World® Resort and Universal Orlando Resort offer reservations-only character meals inside their theme parks *and* at their resort hotels (hotel dining does not require theme-park admission). With few exceptions, these are not fine-dining experiences, nor are they intimate affairs – they can be rather loud and chaotic. Characters rotate around the room, stopping for a minute or so at each table to pose for a photograph and sign autographs. Meals are served buffet-style, family-style or pre-plated, depending on the venue.

Character Experiences

Meet-and-greets inside the theme parks are called 'character experiences,' and they range from simple spots where characters hang out, to small performances. At Disney, there are dozens of characters at spots throughout all four theme parks; at Universal Orlando Resort, you'll find characters ranging from Curious George and Popeye to Lucille Ball and Marilyn Monroe inside both Islands of Adventure and Universal Studios. Check park maps for times and locations.

Best Character Meals

Cinderella's Royal Table The only way inside the iconic castle. (p150)

Akershus Royal Banquet Hall Disney princesses and Norwegian fare. (p52)

Best Character Experiences

Chip 'n' Dale Campfire Singalong Small, low key and laid-back, with s'mores and a Disney movie. (p55)

Enchanted Tales with Belle Charming storytelling performance in Maurice's cottage. (p25)

Meet Gaston Swing by to watch Gaston banter with his fans. (p26)

Best Self-Paced Experiences

Interactive Wands at Wizarding World of Harry Potter Magic wands activate windows, spill water and make trouble. (p71)

Sorcerers of the Magic Kingdom Elaborate park-wide game with hidden clues and secret symbols attracts all ages. (p28)

LAUREL A EGAN/SHUTTERSTOCK ©

Wizarding World of Harry Potter (p61), Universal Studios

Best Shows

Monsters, Inc Laugh Floor Comedy show hosted by on-screen monsters. (p28)

Hoop-Dee-Doo Musical Revue Singing and dancing Vaudeville-style. (p56)

Mickey's Backyard Barbecue Whooping fun with Mickey, Goofy and Donald. (p56)

Best
Eating

There are plenty of restaurants catering to tourists in Lake Buena Vista and Kissimmee, and along International Drive near Universal Orlando Resort, but it's mostly chains and over-hyped disappointments. Restaurant Row (p83) clusters good options in International Dr together, and if you're looking for a quiet escape in the Disney area, head to Celebration. Several restaurants and bars line the small lake there, and they all have patio dining.

Field to Fork

The hum of the field-to-fork Orlando dining scene has developed into a strong and steady crescendo, making it easy to find locally sourced, creatively inspired and delicious food in a city that has built a reputation as a dark hole of national chains, fast food and overpriced theme-park fare. Craft cocktails and artisan beers are an important part of the experience, and it's not just for foodies or fat wallets.

Themed Dining

At Walt Disney World® Resort and Universal Orlando Resort, in both the parks and the entertainment districts, it's less about the food than it is about the experience. Sure, you'll find some excellent meals, and the parks have been trying harder to incorporate fresh, healthy and creative cooking into their menus, but the food can be second to the magic of being transported into a different time and place, or into a different world altogether.

☑ **Top Tips**

▶ If a restaurant is located within a theme park at Walt Disney World® Resort or at Universal Orlando Resort, you must have theme park admission.

▶ Make reservations for Disney dining at www.disneyworld. disney.go.com or My Disney Experience; many restaurants outside the parks let you make reservations on Open Table (www.opentable. com).

Best Field to Fork

Luma on Park Foodie hot spot with seasonal delights and sidewalk seating in Winter Park. (p107)

Ethos Vegan Kitchen Casual vegan spot with

craft brews and good, student vibe. (p103)

Ravenous Pig Locally sourced food and a seasonal menu in Winter Park. (p106)

Best Themed Dining

Sci-Fi Dine-In Theater Science-fiction flicks and a retro menu at Hollywood Studios. (p39)

50's Prime Time Café Grandma's kitchen c 1954. (p41)

Three Broomsticks Pumpkin juice and cottage pie in wizard surrounds. (p71)

Be Our Guest Eat French onion soup and coq au vin in the Beast's castle. (p25)

Yak and Yeti Noodles, dumplings and icy Tsing Tao at the foot of Mt Everest. (p35)

Best Fine Dining at Resort Hotels

Mama Della's Ristorante Romantic and cozy, with tableside serenading and home-style Italian. (p71)

Jiko - The Cooking Place African food, elephants and giraffes outside; extensive wine list. (p50)

Narcoossee's Serenity and romance minutes from Magic Kingdom. (p52)

California Grill Fine dining with rooftop views of Magic Kingdom. (p48)

Best Sweets

Croissant Gourmet French pastries rival the best you'll find in Paris. (p102)

Florean Fortescue's Ice-Cream Parlour Spoon into flavors such as Butterbeer and chocolate chili. (p72)

Toothsome Chocolate Emporium At CityWalk. (p71)

Best Buffet

Boma At Disney's Animal Kingdom Lodge. (p49)

Best for Families

'Ohana At Disney's Polynesian Resort. (p50)

Best View

California Grill At Disney's Contemporary Resort. (p48)

Best Peace & Quiet

Narcoossee's At Disney's Grand Floridian Resort. (p52)

Best in General

Jiko - The Cooking Place At Disney's Animal Kingdom Lodge. (p50)

Slate Contemporary American eats in Restaurant Row. (p83)

Urbain 40 Classy 1940s-style brasserie in Restaurant Row. (p83)

Tutto Gusto Authentic Italian brasserie-cum-wine bar in Epcot. (p49)

Jungle Navigation Co. Ltd Skipper Canteen Adventure-themed eatery in the Magic Kingdom. (p50)

Worth a Trip

The quirky little residential pocket of **Audubon Park** (www.audubonpark gardens.com), just south of Winter Park and centered around the intersection of Corrine Dr and Winter Park Rd, has a distinct urban-hip meets granola-crunchy vibe and offers a handful of recommended restaurants, bakeries and bars. Don't miss the farm-to-table hotspot **East End Market** (www.eastendmkt.com) and **Red Light, Red Light Beer Parlour** (www.redlightredlightbeerparlour.com).

Best
Drinking & Nightlife

Orlando *really* likes to drink, so whether your tastes lean toward a flight of wine at a sidewalk cafe, shots of tequila at a pulsing nightclub or a rooftop Old Fashioned, you'll be satisfied. Head to CityWalk (p76) or downtown Orlando for the greatest concentration of clubs and live music, and to Winter Park or Thornton Park for low-key imbibing.

PHOTOSOUNDS/SHUTTERSTOCK ©

In the Theme Parks

Drinking in the theme parks is all about the theming – sipping fresh lime juice mojitos in Africa, Wizard's Brew in Diagon Alley or a flight of scotch at the Hollywood Brown Derby. Excepting Magic Kingdom, you'll find bars inside all the parks.

Craft Cocktail Bars

Exacting attention to quality spirits, fresh ingredients and vintage recipes define Orlando's craft cocktail scene. While the theme park and International Drive tourist centers have joined the cocktail craze, and there's excellent sipping to be found everywhere, low-key neighborhood spots pepper greater Orlando.

Best Themed Bars

La Cava del Tequila Avocado margarita with a salsa trio in Mexico. (p53)

Hog's Head Pub Shady spot of disrepute, frequented by wizards of questionable character. (p76)

Moe's Tavern Homer's favorite dive with all the color and detail from the show. (p61)

Icebar (p85) Icy seats, drinks and bar.

Strong Water Tavern (p75) Caribbean rums and tapas.

Best Local Drinking

Courtesy Bar Unpretentious craft cocktails and vintage surrounds. (p88)

Woods Post-work favorite for cocktails and craft brew. (p94)

Hanson's Shoe Repair Prohibition-style speakeasy with rooftop patio and twinkle lights. (p93)

Best
For Free

Though part of the Disney magic is how it makes your money disappear, and all the theme parks will lighten your wallet considerably, there are a handful of free highlights in and around Orlando. In addition, the tourist hubs of CityWalk and Downtown Disney both offer eye-candy and street-energy, and they don't require theme park admission.

NADEZDA MURMAKOVA/SHUTTERSTOCK ©

Chip 'n' Dale Campfire Singalong Singing with chipmunks, campfires and a Disney film. (p55)

Nighttime Spectacular Watch the fireworks over Magic Kingdom's Cinderella's Castle. (p25)

Disney's BoardWalk Echoes turn-of-the-century New England seaside resorts, with weekend magicians, jugglers and musicians. (p47)

Popcorn Flicks in the Park Casablanca, Vertigo, cult classics and more, screened in Winter Park's grassy Central Park. (p109)

Orlando Farmers Market Crafts, food and an outdoor beer garden. (p94)

Winter Park Farmers Market Neighborhood market in a historic train depot. (p107)

CityWalk Beating the heat in the splash fountain. (p76)

Lake Eola Park Orlando's pretty downtown park is perfect for a leisurely post-lunch stroll. (p91)

☑ **Top Tips**

▶ Orlando Grocery Express (www.orlandogroceryexpress.com) and Garden Grocer (www.gardengrocer.com) deliver groceries, beer and wine to your hotel or rental home.

▶ If you're staying at Disney or Universal resort hotel, ask about free family-friendly movies screened poolside.

▶ For free event listings, including outdoor movie screenings and festivals, in and around Orlando, visit http://orlandoonthecheap.com.

Best
Ways to Relax

Crowds, noise, stomach-churning coasters and in-your-face special effects, lines for food, lines for rides and lines for bathrooms, stand-still traffic, parking shuttles and packed Disney buses... Orlando can be exhausting and stressful. Though it's hard to find a quiet spot in and around the theme parks, and Orlando city sprawl can feel defeating, we have some favorite spots to relax.

CHICAGO TRIBUNE/GETTY IMAGES ©

Best At Walt Disney World® Resort

Belle Vue Room Play a game of cards on the 2nd-floor garden-view balcony. (p53)

Disney's BoardWalk Stroll along the path between Epcot and Disney's Hollywood Studios to this low-key seaside-resort-themed area. (p47)

Narcoossee's Dine at the Grand Floridian, or just come for a glass of wine on the pier. (p52)

Mickey's PhilharMagic The lines rarely get long at this air-conditioned 3D classic. (p25)

Disney's Enchanted Tiki Room You can walk in and out whenever you like and it's never crowded. (p43)

It's a Small World A slow cruise through the world offers welcome calm. (p43)

Best Beyond Disney

Mama Della's Ristorante Escape into a cozy Italian home for home-cooking and a glass of Chianti. (p71)

Emeril's Tchoup Chop Sophisticated Asian-inspired fare with low-key elegance. (p72)

Winter Park Pedestrian friendly small town offers an oasis in city sprawl. (p98)

Orlando Farmers Market Beer garden, local produce and food stalls on the shores of Lake Eola. (p94)

☑ Top Tips

► Head to Disney's Grand Floridian for a break from Magic Kingdom. The four-story lobby, with a live orchestra playing jazz (and yes, Disney classics), oozes old Florida style, and tiny tot TV-watching areas play Disney cartoons.

► To get to the Grand Floridian from Magic Kingdom, hop on a boat and get off at the first stop; to get back to Magic Kingdom, hop on the monorail – Magic Kingdom is the first stop.

Best
Entertainment

Best on Stage

Cirque du Soleil La Nouba (p55) Disney's best live show.

Mad Cow Theatre Indie downtown theater house. (p89)

Orlando Philharmonic Orchestra (https://orlandophil.org) Classics, pop, opera and more.

John & Rita Lowndes Shakespeare Center Three theaters stage first-rate performances. (p97)

Best Comedy

Blue Man Group Percussion-driven explosion of the senses with audience participation. (p77)

SAK Comedy Lab Intimate interactive comedy improv. (p95)

Best Live Music

House of Blues Swing by on Sunday for the Gospel brunch. (p56)

Velvet Bar Leopard-skin cocktail lounge, sultry tunes and Hard Rock hotel energy. (p75)

Tanqueray's Downtown Orlando Local music in a smoky basement dive. (p94)

The Social Orlando institution brings big names to its tiny space. (p95)

TESTA IMAGES/GETTY IMAGES ©

☑ Top Tips

▶ For a complete listing of performing arts, organized by category and date, and ticket purchasing, visit Orlando Theater (www.orlando-theater.com).

▶ Orlando Venues (www.orlandovenues.net) sells tickets for theater, live-music and sporting events at venues throughout Orlando.

Best
Shopping

Theme park souvenirs, kitschy must-haves, outlet shopping and indoor malls with all the national chains define Orlando shopping, and Disney's MagicBand room-charge makes it particularly easy to shop inside its parks. With the exception of Winter Park, farmers markets, and small stretches scattered throughout the city, this is not the place for leisurely shopping strolls, local art and serendipitous discoveries.

CHIP LITHERLAND PHOTOGRAPHY INC ©

☑ **Top Tip**

▶ Merchandise purchased at Disney and Universal theme parks can be delivered to a designated location at the park entrance for pick-up as you exit; if you're staying at a resort hotel, it can be delivered directly to your room. Allow several hours for delivery.

Theme Park Souvenirs

While there are endless stores throughout the parks, don't expect to find the same things in all the parks and resorts. Most stores are thematically oriented so near the Winnie-the- Pooh ride you'll find lots of bear stuff; and after the Indiana Jones ride you'll find, well, an *Indiana Jones* fedora, of course. For a one-stop shop, Disney Springs (p54) has the largest Disney character store in the country with 12 massive rooms choc-a-block with everything you can imagine.

Best Souvenirs

Wizarding World of Harry Potter – Diagon Alley Magical windows, Fishy Green Ale and quidditch robes. (p61)

World of Disney The country's largest store for everything Disney. (p57)

Main Street, USA Mouse-ear Rice Krispies, crystal Donald Ducks and princess-themed everything. (p46)

Lego Imagination Center Life-sized Lego sculptures plus a wall of individually priced Lego pieces. (p57)

Best Local Shopping

Lighten Up Toy Store Puzzles, classic games, kites and books. (p109)

Rifle Paper Co Handmade paper studio and artisan gifts. (p109)

Rocket Fizz Hundreds of sodas and candy from around the world. (p109)

Peterbrooke Chocolatier of Winter Park High-end chocolate boutique. (p109)

Best
Art & Culture

While arts and culture don't take front stage in Orlando tourist attractions, a vibrant indie scene simmers beyond the visitor hubs of Disney and International Drive. In addition to galleries, museums and weekly events, annual festivals enjoy stellar reputations.

GLOWIMAGES/GETTY IMAGES ©

Best Galleries & Museums

Orlando Museum of Art Grand dame of the Orlando art scene. (p97)

Charles Hosmer Morse Museum of American Art The world's largest collection of Louis Comfort Tiffany art and recreated rooms from his Long Island estate. (p100)

Mennello Museum of American Art Intimate lakeside space with a focus on folk art. (p97)

Orange County Regional History Center

Period recreations and changing displays examine the Orlando history and culture. (p91)

Best Festivals

Orlando International Fringe Festival (www. orlandofringe.org)

Florida Film Festival (www.floridafilmfestival. com)

Zora! Festival (www. zorafestival.org)

Winter Park Sidewalk Art Festival (www. wpsaf.org)

☑ **Top Tips**

▶ The free Orlando Weekly (www.orlan doweekly.com) and Axis (https:// orlando-axis.com) have comprehensive listings of the city's music, entertainment and bar scene.

▶ Orlando Arts Magazine (http:// unitedarts.cc/ magazine) is the city's go-to source for arts, culture and events. The biggest and best art festivals include the Winter Park Sidewalk Art Festival in mid-March and the Orlando International Fringe Festival in May.

Best
Outdoor Activities

After a few days of theme-park rides and lines, fried food, loud music, traffic and shopping, a jaunt beyond the pavement can soothe and rejuvenate even the most harried of spirits.

ADVENTURES ON WHEELS/SHUTTERSTOCK ©

Parks & Gardens

Harry P Leu Gardens The ideal place for a picnic and lesson in the art of growing camelias. In Audubon Park. (www.leugardens.org)

Lake Eola Park Orlando's pretty downtown park is perfect for a leisurely post-lunch stroll. (p91)

Wekiwa Springs State Park Cool off in the swimming hole, hike miles of trails and paddle the tranquil waters of the Wekiva River. (www.floridastateparks.org/wekiwasprings)

Golf

Grand Cypress Golf Club Beautiful 45 holes just outside Walt Disney World®. (www.grandcypress.com)

Disney's Lake Buena Vista Golf Course Championship golf

course with elevated bunkered greens. (www.golfwdw.com)

Disney's Palm Golf Course Picturesque 18-hole championship course. (p48)

On the Water

Central Florida Nature Adventures Kayak alongside alligators, turtles and egrets. (www.kayakcentralflorida.com)

Kelly Park Rent an inner tube and float along a shallow stream, 20 miles northwest of downtown Orlando. (www.ocfl.net/cultureparks)

Buena Vista Watersports Just outside the Disney gates, with a low-key vibe. (www.bvwatersports.com)

Sammy Duvall's Watersports Centre Lessons, rentals and parasailing. (www.sammyduvall.com)

☑ **Top Tips**

▶ Orlando boasts more than 60 golf courses. For details and packages, go to www.golfpacorlando.com.

▶ For maps of Orlando's paved bike trails, visit www.orlandosentinel.com/travel/bike-trails.

Cycling

Breakaway Bikes Rent a bike for a scenic ride around Winter Park. (p143)

West Orange Trail Bikes & Blades For rentals and information, 20 miles west of Orlando, at the beginning of the West Orange Trail. (www.orlandobikerental.com)

Survival Guide

Survival Guide

Before You Go

When to Go

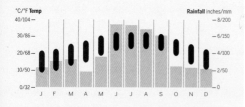

°C/°F Temp
40/104 —
30/86 —
20/68 —
10/50 —
0/32 —

Rainfall inches/mm
— 8/200
— 6/150
— 4/100
— 2/50
— 0

J F M A M J J A S O N D

➡ **Winter (Dec–Feb)**
Christmas through early
January draws massive
theme-park crowds.
Otherwise, low-season
bargains abound as
temps can dip below
freezing.

➡ **Spring (Mar–May)**
March to April is peak
tourism season thanks to
spring breakers. Crowds
thin and prices drop in
May.

➡ **Summer (Jun–Aug)**
Busy with summer
holiday crowds, lots of
festivals. Hot, humid,
90-degree-plus
temperatures.

➡ **Autumn (Sep–Nov)**
The masses diminish
after Labor Day, except
for Halloween festivities.
Lodging prices plummet
and summer sizzle fades.

Book Your Stay

☑ Expect to pay $25 to
$50 on top of the quoted
price for a hotel room at re
sorts and boutique hotels.
Most charge for parking
and wi-fi, and add a hefty
'resort fee'.

Useful Websites

Lonely Planet (www.
lonelyplanet.com) Writer-
recommended reviews
and online booking.

ReserveOrlando (www.
reserveorlando.com) Cen-
tral booking agency.

Orlando Visitors Center
(www.visitorlando.com)
Options from the tour-
ism office's jam-packed
website.

**Orlando Vacation Home
Rental** (www.orlando
-vacationhomerental.com)
Predominantly gated com-
munity homes.

**Universal Orlando Re-
sort** (www.universal
orlando.com) On-site

...otels at Universal Orlando Resort.

...IS (www.wdwinfo.com) Loads of details and ...hotos of Walt Disney World® and Lake Buena Vista hotels.

Best Budget

Disney's Fort Wilderness Resort (☎407-939-...277, 407-824-2900; www. ...isneyworld.disney.go.com; ...510 N Fort Wilderness Trail; ...ent sites $76, RV sites $97-...22, 6-person cabins $359; ❄@🛜⛱🐾; 🚌Disney, ⛴Disney) Cabins and ...ampground in a natural ...reserve. Has nightly ...ampfire singalongs.

Courtyard at Lake ...ucerne (☎407-648-5188; ...ww.orlandohistoricinn. ...om; 211 N Lucerne Circle E, ...owntown; r incl breakfast ...rom $140; P❄🛜) Lovely, ...pacious B&B in a his-...oric home in Downtown ...rlando.

Floridian Hotel & Suites (☎407-212-3021; www.florid ...anhotelorlando.com; 7531 ...anada Ave, International Dr; ...from $75; P❄⊛🛜⛱) Wonderful, privately ...wned hotel with spotless ...ooms and complimen-...ary breakfast.

Best Midrange

Hyatt Regency Grand Cypress Resort (☎800-233-1234, 407-239-1234; www.hyattgrandcypress. com; 1 Grand Cypress Blvd, Lake Buena Vista; r $189-250, resort fee per day $30, self/valet parking $20/29; P@🛜⛱🐾) Quality rooms, service, grounds and amenities, 7 miles from Disney's Magic Kingdom.

Walt Disney World Swan & Dolphin Hotels (☎Dolphin 407-934-4000, Swan 407-934-3000; www. swandolphin.com; 1200 & 1500 Epcot Resorts Blvd; r $160-380; P❄@🛜⛱; 🚌Disney, ⛴Disney) Two high-rise luxury hotels with a distinctly toned-down Disney feel but all the Disney perks.

Hilton Orlando Bonnet Creek (☎407-597-3600; www.hiltonbonnetcreek.com; 14100 Bonnet Creek Resort Lane, Greater Orlando; r from $210, resort fee per day $30, self/valet parking $22/30; P@🛜⛱) Big pool with lazy river, and surrounded by Walt Disney World® Resort, but without the mayhem.

Cabana Bay Beach Resort (☎407-503-4000; www.universalorlando.com; 6550 Adventure Way, Universal Orlando Resort; r $149-172, parking $12; P❄🛜⛱; 🚌Universal) Family suites and early access to Wizarding World of Harry Potter.

Disney's Coronado Springs Resort (☎407-939-5277, 407-939-1000; www.disneyworld. disney.go.com; 1000 W Buena Vista Dr; r from $210; P❄@🛜⛱; 🚌Disney) Southwestern theme with a low-key tone that sets it apart from other Disney hotels.

Best Top End

Loews Portofino Bay Hotel (☎407-503-1000; www.loewshotels.com/ portofino-bay-hotel; 5601 Universal Blvd, Universal Orlando Resort; r & ste $325-$390, self/valet parking per day $22/30; P❄@🛜⛱🐾; ⛴Universal) Elegantly evokes the relaxing charm of seaside Italy.

Bay Hill Club and Lodge (☎407-876-2429, 888-422-9455; www.bayhill.com; 9000 Bay Hill Blvd; r from $300; @🛜⛱) Reassuringly

Walt Disney World® Resort Hotels

Disney resort hotels are divided according to location (Magic Kingdom, Epcot, Animal Kingdom and Disney Boardwalk). Prices vary drastically according to season, week and day.

Disney's website www.disneyworld.disney.go.com outlines all its resorts and package offerings. Most rooms sleep up to four, with no extra charge for children or cribs, and a handful offer themed rooms and bunk beds.

While deluxe resorts are the best Disney has to offer, note that you're paying for Disney theming and location convenience, not luxury. Most offer multiroom suites and villas, upscale restaurants, children's programs and easy access to theme parks. Epcot resorts offer walking access and pleasant boat transport to restaurants and entertainment at Disney's Board-Walk, Hollywood Studios and Epcot, while Magic Kingdom resorts are an easy boat or monorail ride to park gates.

Five value resorts, the least-expensive Disney properties available (not including camping), have thousands of motel-style rooms and suites; are decorated according to their theme; connect to all the parks by bus only; and cater to families and traveling school groups. You will definitely feel the difference because of the lower price: instead of proper restaurants, there are food courts and snack bars, and things are particularly bright, hectic and loud. Some value resorts offer family suites with two bathrooms and a kitchenette.

Staying Around Walt Disney World®

If you don't stay in a Walt Disney World® resort, countless other hotels, motels and resorts in Lake Buena Vista, Kissimmee and Celebration lie within a few miles of Walt Disney World®. There's an excellent selection of chain motels along grassy Palm Pkwy just outside Disney's gates and a cluster of seven upscale chain hotels (www.downtowndisneyhotels.com) across from Disney Springs.

Universal Orlando Resort Hotels

Universal Orlando Resort boasts five excellent resort hotels. Staying at a resort eliminates many logistical hassles: it's a pleasant gardened walk or a quiet boat ride to the parks; most offer Unlimited Express Pass access to park attractions and priority dining; several popular rides, such as Wizarding World of Harry Potter, opens one hour early for all guests; and the Loews Loves Pets program welcomes Fido as a VIP.

alm and simple. Gracious staff and handsome rooms.

Legoland Hotel (1 Legoland Way, Winter Haven; r from $420; P ❋ ☎) Excellently themed hotel with treasure hunts and lego workshops.

Four Seasons Resort Orlando at Walt Disney World (☎ 800-267-3046; www.fourseasons.com; 10100 Dream Tree Blvd; r/ste from $435/430; P ❋ @ ☎ ☀) All the luxury, quality and attention to detail you'd expect from a Four Seasons resort.

Alfond Inn (☎ 407-998-8090; www.thealfondinn.com; 300 E New England Ave; r from $309; ❋ @ ☎ ☀) Boutique hotel with a welcoming vibe in Winter Park.

Arriving in Orlando

Orlando International Airport

Disney's Magical Express (☎ 866-599-0951; www.disneyworld.

disney.go.com) If you're staying at a Disney hotel, arrange in advance for complimentary luggage handling and deluxe bus transportation.

Orlando Airport Towncar (☎ 800-532-8563, 407-754-8166; www.orlandoairport-towncar.com) Town car to Lake Buena Vista (25 minutes) costs one-way/return $60/120 for up to four people; an SUV for up to six costs one way/return $85/170. It's about $15 less for transport to the Universal Orlando Resort area.

Legacy Towncar of Orlando (☎ 407-695-4413, 888-939-8227; www.legacytowncar.com) Prices include a 20-minute grocery stop. Town car to Lake Buena Vista costs one-way/return $70/120 for up to four people; passenger van for up to 10 costs one way/return $85/155. For 11 to 14 people, they'll add a luggage trailer to the van (one way $35).

Mears Transportation (☎ 855-463-2776) Call one day in advance to arrange personalized transport between a long list of hotels and many attrac-

tions, including Universal Orlando Resort and SeaWorld. It costs between $21 to $29 per round trip per person.

Casablanca Transportation (☎ 407-927-2773, www.casablancatransportation.com) provides good service to the airport and in and around Orlando.

Lynx (☎ 407-841-2279, route info 407-841-8240; www.golynx.com; 455 Garland Ave, Downtown; per ride/day/week $2/4.50/16, transfers free; ⏰ call center 8am-8pm Mon-Fri, 8am-6pm Sat & Sun) Located in Terminal A. Bus 42 to International Drive runs from 5:40am to 10pm Monday through Saturday, and from 6:30am to 9pm Sunday. It's a one-hour ride.

Taxi Rides to Lake Buena Vista and Universal Orlando Resort area take 25 to 35 minutes (depending on traffic) and cost $55 to $70.

Orlando Sanford International Airport

Orlando Airport Towncar Greets you at baggage claim. Town car transport to Lake Buena Vista costs one way/return $90/175 for one to four people and takes about an hour, but larger transport is not available. It's about $5 less for transport to the Universal Orlando Resort area.

Legacy Towncar of Orlando Prices include a 20-minute grocery stop. Town car transport to Lake Buena Vista costs one way/return $100/185 for up to four people and takes about an hour. Passenger van for up to 10 costs one way/return $140/240.

Taxi Rides to Lake Buena Vista take an hour and cost $120 to $130; to the Universal Orlando Resort area, it costs $85 to $100 and takes about 40 minutes.

From Amtrak Stations

Amtrak's 97 Silver Meteor and 91 Silver Star from New York to Miami stop at Winter Park, downtown Orlando and Kissimmee. It's about a 22-hour ride from NYC (from $140). The daily Auto Train from Lorton, VA, terminates at Sanford, 30 miles north of downtown Orlando.

Orlando Station Full-service station with Hertz car rental and a taxi stand. It's about 30 minutes to Walt Disney World®.

Kissimmee Station Staffed station about 25 minutes east of Walt Disney World®. No car rental. Call ☎407-222-2222 for a taxi.

Winter Park Station Staffed 8am to 9pm. Sun-Rail stops here. No car rental. Call for a taxi.

Sanford Station Unstaffed station about an hour's drive to Walt Disney World®. Hertz offers rental cars, but you need to reserve a car in advance and call upon arrival; a shuttle will pick you up. Call for a taxi.

Getting Around

Disney Transportation

➡ Disney boats, mono-rails and buses connect every sight and resort hotel within Walt Disney World® Resort, but not everything is directly connected.

➡ Allow yourself at least one hour to get from point A to B; transport to Magic Kingdom from Magic Kingdom resorts can be much less, and some routes can be much more.

➡ Three separate mono-rail routes service select locations within Walt Disney World® Resort, including the Transportation & Ticket Center, Magic Kingdom and Magic Kingdom resort hotels (Disney's Poly-nesian, Grand Floridian and Contemporary), and Epcot.

➡ There is no Disney transportation from Downtown Disney directly to the theme parks.

➡ If you have a dining reservation at Disney's Polynesian, Grand Florid-ian or Contemporary Resorts, you can park for free; from there, it is an easy monorail or boat to Magic Kingdom.

➡ Avoid Disney buses and the Transportation & Ticket Center during busy imes and seasons. Waits can be long and crowds can be overwhelming.

Universal Orlando Resort Transportation

➡ Boats connect CityWalk and theme parks to deluxe resorts; they run from one hour before early admission to Wizarding World of Harry Potter to 2:30am.

➡ To get to the theme parks from Cabana Bay, you must take a five-minute shuttle to the transportation hub, and then walk 10 minutes through CityWalk.

Car & Motorcycle

☑ **Best for...**Exploring Orlando beyond the theme parks.

➡ Car rentals range from $80 to $400 per week, plus sales tax and insurance.

➡ If driving to Magic Kingdom, you must park at the TTC, catch a tram to the transport hub, and then hop on a ferry or monorail to theme park gates.

➡ Parking at Disney theme parks and Universal Orlando Resort costs $20.

➡ Budget and midrange hotels usually don't charge for parking, but resorts charge $20 to $25 per day; often valet only.

I-Ride Trolley

☑ **Best for...**Sights, restaurants, bars and accommodation along International Dr.

➡ Buy one-day ($5) and multiday (from $7 for three days) tickets at hotels and sights along International Dr.

➡ Only exact fare, in cash, is accepted on board ($2).

➡ To get to Universal Orlando Resort, get off at Universal's Volcano Bay and walk 15 minutes over the interstate.

Taxi

☑ **Best for...**Time-saving ease.

➡ If taking a taxi to Magic Kingdom, ask to be dropped off at the Contemporary Resort; from here, it is an easy five-minute walk to the gates of Magic Kingdom. Otherwise, they drop you off at the Transportation & Ticket Center and you must take a ferry or monorail to the park.

SunRail

☑ **Best for...**Reaching Winter Park, Loch Haven Park, downtown Orlando, and Thornton Park.

➡ North–south running commuter rail (www.sunrail.com) runs Monday to Friday.

➡ Convenient stops include Winter Park (downtown Winter Park), Florida Hospital Health Village (Loch Haven Park) and Church St (downtown Orlando).

➡ Tickets range from $2 to $7.50 one way/return.

Bicycle

☑ **Best for...**Getting around Winter Park.

Breakaway Bikes (Map p104; 407-622-2453; www.breakawaybicycleswinterpark.com; 141 Lincoln Ave; per hour/day $10/35; 10am-6pm Tue-Sat, 11am-5pm Sun) Ask for their Scenic Bike Ride map.

Walt Disney World Bicycle Rental (407-939-7529; www.disneyworld.disney.go.com; select Walt Disney World® resorts; per hr/day $9/18, surrey bikes per 30min from $25) More than a dozen bike-rental places throughout Walt Disney World® rent on a

Walt Disney World® Resort Tickets

One-day tickets Valid for admission to Magic Kingdom. Separate one-day tickets at slightly lower prices are valid for admission to Epcot, Hollywood Studios or Animal Kingdom.

Multiday tickets Valid for one theme park per day for each day of the ticket (you can leave/reenter the park but cannot enter another park).

Park Hopper Gives same-day admission to any/all of the four Walt Disney World® parks. Fair warning: hopping between four parks requires a lot of stamina. Two parks a day is more feasible.

Park Hopper Plus The same as Park Hopper, but you can toss in Blizzard Beach, Typhoon Lagoon and Oak Trail Golf Course.

Days	Multiday Prices (age 10+/ age 3-9)	Park Hopper (age 10+/ age 3-9)	Park Hopper Plus (age 10+/ age 3-9)
2	$199/187	$259/247	$274/262
3	$289/271	$349/331	$364/346
4	$350/330	$425/405	$440/420
5	$370/350	$445/425	$460/440
6	$390/370	$465/445	$480/460
7	$410/390	$485/465	$500/480
8	$420/400	$495/475	$510/490
9	$430/410	$505/485	$520/500
10	$440/420	$515/495	$530/510

Disney Dining Offers Complex Disney Dining Plans are available to guests of Disney resort hotels; see www.disneyworld.disney.go.com for prices.

Buying tickets Buying at the gate is $20 more expensive than online.

first-come, first-served basis.

Orange Cycle (☎407-422-5552; www.orange-cycleorlando.com; 2204 Edgewater Dr; ◷10am-7pm Mon-Fri, 10am-5pm Sat)

Provides printable maps to Orlando bike trails and is an excellent source of information for all things biking in and around Orlando. Sells and repairs bikes, but does not rent.

Tours

Note that tours inside theme parks require theme park admission in addition to the cost of the tour.

Disney Tours (📞407-939-8687, VIP tours 407-560-4033; www.disneyworld. disney.go.com; Walt Disney World®; prices vary) Offers all kinds of guided tours and specialty experiences, including a **VIP tour** ($400 to $600 per hour per group of up to 10 people) with front-of-the-line access.

Keys to the Kingdom (📞407-939-8687; www. disneyworld.disney.go; Magic Kingdom; tours $99, theme-park admission required; 🕐8am, 8:30am, 9am & 9:30am) This popular five-hour tour peeks into the Magic Kingdom's underground tunnels and backstage secrets – no children allowed, so as not to destroy the magic!

Universal Orlando Resort Tickets

Tickets for adults to one or both Universal Orlando Resort Parks (Islands of Adventure and Universal Studios) cost the following:

No of Days	One Park ($) adult/child	Two Parks ($) adult/child
1	105/100	155/150
2	185/175	235/225
3	204/195	260/245
4	215/205	265/255

➡ Tickets are good anytime within 14 consecutive days, and multiple-day tickets include admission to paid venues in CityWalk. Universal Orlando Resort participates in the Orlando Flex Ticket available online or in person at the Orlando **Official Visitor Center** (Map p80; 📞407-363-5872; www.visitorlando.com; 8723 International Dr; 🕐8:30am-6pm; 🚃I-Ride Trolley Red Line 15).

➡ **Express Pass** Avoid lines at designated Islands of Adventure and Universal Studios rides by flashing your Express Pass at the separate Express Pass line. The standard one-day pass (for one park $50 to $60; for two parks from $65) allows one-time Express Pass access to each attraction. Alternatively, purchase the bundled two-day Park-to-Park Ticket Plus Unlimited Express (from $220), which includes admission to both parks and unlimited access to Express Pass rides. With this, you can go to any ride, any time you like, as often as you like. If you are staying at one of Universal Orlando's deluxe resort hotels – Universal Orlando's Loews Portofino Bay, Hard Rock or Loews Royal Pacific Resort – up to five guests in each room automatically receive an Unlimited Express Pass. A limited number of passes per day are available online or at the park gates. Check www.universalorlando.com for a calendar of prices and black-out dates.

➡ A three-day, three-park ticket (two to five days duration) to Volcano Bay costs from $245/235.

My Disney Experience: FastPass & MagicBand

FastPass+ is designed to allow guests to plan their days in advance and reduce time spent waiting in line. Visitors can reserve a specific time for up to three attractions per day through My Disney Experience (www.disneyworld. disney.go.com), accessible online or by downloading the free mobile app. There are also kiosks in each park where you can make reservations.

Resort guests receive a **MagicBand** – a plastic wristband that serves as a room key, park entrance ticket, FastPass+ access and room charge. As soon as you make your room reservation, you can set up your My Disney Experience account and begin planning your day-by-day Disney itinerary. Your itinerary, including any changes you make online or through the mobile app, will automatically be stored in your wristband.

Once at the park, head to your reserved FastPass+ ride or attraction anytime within the preselected one-hour timeframe. Go to the Fastpass+ entrance, scan your MagicBand and zip right onto the attraction with no more than a 15-minute wait. Though it's a simple system, there are some kinks, so a few tips can help you navigate it smoothly with optimal benefit.

➡ If you are staying at a Disney Resort, you can access My Disney Experience and start reserving FastPass+ attractions up to 60 days in advance; nonresort guests with purchased theme-park tickets can reserve FastPass+ attractions 30 days in advance.

➡ You can use Fastpass+ selections for rides, character greeting spots (where lines can rival the most popular rides), fireworks, parades and shows.

➡ Some parks use a tiered FastPass+ system – you must choose one attraction from group one and two from group two.

➡ Make reservations for meals and character dining through My Disney Experience.

➡ Do not waste your limited FastPass+ options on attractions that do not have long lines; carefully consider your day's plan to maximize the benefits of this system. Disney planning websites offer all kinds of tips. At the Magic Kingdom, lines for Seven Dwarf's Mine Train, Peter Pan's Flight, Big Thunder Mountain Railroad, Enchanted Tales with Belle and Space Mountain can be painfully long. Use your FastPass+ for sequential afternoon times at three of these and use the morning, when your patience and energy is stronger and the lines are shorter, for other attractions.

➡ Check the website or call for updated information, as the system is always in flux.

Essential Information

Childcare

Disney's Children Activity Center (📞407-939-3463; www.disneyworld.disney.com.go; select Disney resort hotels; per child per hr $12, 2hr minimum, incl dinner; ⏱hours vary) Five Disney resorts offer excellent drop-off children's activity centers for children aged three to 14, with organized activities, toys, art supplies, meals and a Disney movie in the evening. Reservations required but you do not have to be a hotel guest to use the centers.

Kid's Nite Out (📞407-828-0920, freecall 1-800-696-8105; www.kidsniteout.com; 1/2/3/4/5 kids per hr $18//21/24/26/28, 4hr minimum, plus travel fee $10; ⏱sitters available 24/7) Walt Disney World® uses Kid's Nite Out for private in-room child care for children ages six months to 12 years. You can also hire a helper if you need an extra pair of hands when you're out

and about, but note that you'll have to pay the caregiver's theme park ticket.

Kids' Camp (📞Hard Rock 407-503-2200, Loews Portofino Bay 407-503-1200, Loews Royal Pacific 407-503-3200; www.universalorlando.com; Universal Orlando; Portofino Bay, Hard Rock & Royal Pacific Resorts; per child per hr $15; ⏱5-11pm Mon-Thu, to midnight Fri & Sat) Every week one deluxe Universal Orlando Resort hotel offers a drop-off child-care center for children aged four through 14. Reservations recommended but not required; you must be a guest at one of the five Universal Orlando Resort hotels. Optional dinner for an extra $15.

Discount Cards

Visit Orlando (Map p80; 📞407-363-5872; www.visitorlando.com; 8723 International Dr; ⏱8:30am-6pm; 🚊I-Ride Trolley Red Line 15) now offers discounts on its website instead of through the Orlando MagiCard. Also keep in mind that Orlando is a *very* competitive tourist destination, so persistence, patience and

thorough research often pays dividends.

Electricity

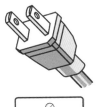

120V/60Hz

120V/60Hz

Emergencies

Police, fire, ambulance:
📞911

Health

Medical Services

Theme parks and resorts all have medical facilities.

Centra Care Walk-In
(📞407-934-2273; www.centracare.org; ⏰8am-midnight Mon-Fri, to 8pm Sat & Sun) Medical Walk-in medical center with more than 20 locations.

Doctors on Call Services
(📞407-399-3627; www.doctorsoncallservice.com; ⏰24hr) Twenty-four-hour doctors on-call to your hotel, including to Walt Disney World® and Universal Orlando Resort.

Internet Access

It is not difficult to get connected in Orlando. All theme parks and many sights offer free connection, as do numerous cafes plus all hotels (though this may be included as part of a 'resort fee'). If somewhere is guests only, ask about public access in hotel lobbies and pools.

Kennels

Only service animals are allowed inside theme parks.

Best Friends Pet Care at Walt Disney World Resort (📞877-493-9738; www.bestfriendspetcare.com/waltdisneyworldresort; 2510 Bonnet Creek Pkwy; per day $18-72, overnight $41-89; ⏰1hr before Walt Disney World® parks open to 1hr after closing) Offers overnight boarding and day care for dogs, cats and 'pocket pets.' Rates vary depending on how many walks and extra perks you'd like, and are a bit less for guests staying at a Disney hotel. Reserva-

tions and written proof of vaccination (DHLPP, rabies and Bordetella for dogs; FVRCP and rabies for cats) are required.

Universal Orlando Resort Kennel (📞407-224-9509; www.universalorlando.com; Universal Orlando Resort; per pet per day $15; ⏰7am-3am) Day boarding for dogs and cats, but you must return to walk your pet. Located on the left side of the RV/camper parking lot at Universal Orlando Resort parking lot. Note that pets are welcome at all on-site hotels except Cabana Bay.

LGBT Travelers

Though it explodes during Gay Days (www.gaydays.com) in June, there is a solid gay and lesbian community in Orlando year-round.

Maps

Walt Disney World® Resort

Park maps with listings of the day's scheduled events and activities (including character meets) are available at the park entrances, Guest Services and all retail

Route Planner

For help navigating the buses, boats and monorail that comprise Disney transportation, go to the Transportation Wizard at www.ourlaughingplace.com. Plug in your start and finish points, and it will tell you the best route and estimated time; also available as the GPS TWiz app ($3).

locations throughout the parks.

Universal Orlando Resort

Pick up a free map at each park entrance (and dotted around the park). They also list the attractions, with a schedule outlining events, shows and locations of free character interactions. The monthly *Times & Info Guide* lists larger parades and events, too.

Money

➡ You will find ATMs throughout Walt Disney World®. Guest Services at each park offer limited currency exchange.

➡ Personal checks not drawn on US banks are generally not accepted.

➡ Exchange foreign currency at international airports and most large banks in Miami, Orlando, Tampa and other cities.

➡ Major credit cards are widely accepted, and they are required for car rentals.

➡ Most ATM withdrawals using out-of-state cards incur surcharges of $3 or so.

Tipping

➡ In restaurants, for satisfactory to excellent service, tipping 15% to 25% of the bill is expected.

➡ Bartenders expect $1 per drink; cafe baristas, put a little change in the jar.

➡ Taxi drivers and hairdressers expect 10% to 15%.

➡ Skycaps (airport porters) and porters at nice hotels expect $1 a bag or so. If you spend several nights in a hotel, it's polite to leave a few dollars for the cleaning staff.

Opening Hours

Theme park hours change seasonally and daily. Generally, parks open at 8am or 9am and close sometime between 6pm and 10pm. Guests at most on-site hotels can enter selected parks one hour before official opening times.

Bars 4pm to 1am or 2am weekdays, 3am on weekends.

Museums 10am to 5:30pm.

Nightclubs 9pm to 1am or 2am weekdays, 3am on weekends.

Strollers

Strollers (single/double per day $15/31, multiday $13/27) are available to rent on a first-come, first-served basis at Disney's four theme parks and Disney Springs, and you can also purchase umbrella strollers.

Restaurants Breakfast 7am or 8am to 11am; lunch 11am or 11:30am to 2:30pm or 3pm; dinner 5pm or 6pm to 10pm Sunday to Thursday, to 11pm or midnight Friday and Saturday.

Shops 10am to 7pm Monday to Saturday, noon to 6pm Sunday.

Theme Parks 9am to 6pm, often later and sometimes as late as 1am; check websites for daily hours.

Public Holidays

Banks, schools, offices and most shops close on these days. Theme parks remain open.

New Year's Day January 1

Meeting Disney Characters

Folks of all ages pay a lot of money and spend hours in line to get their photo taken with Winnie-the-Pooh, Donald Duck, Elsa and other Disney favorites. If this is what makes you swoon (versus just spotting them from a short distance, which can also be fun), see www.disneyworld.disney.go.com. There is a plethora of opportunities to sidle up next to a princess, villain or furry friend. Note that character experiences in the resort hotels do not require theme-park tickets.

Disney Character Dining (☎407-939-3463; https://disneyworld.disney.go.com/dining/#/character-dining; Walt Disney World® theme parks & resort hotels; prices vary) Make reservations up to six months (yes, six!) for any of the 20 or so character-dining meals at Walt Disney World®. They're hardly relaxing and are rather loud and chaotic. Characters stop at each table to pose for a photograph and interact briefly. Disney's **Grand Floridian Resort** (☎407-939-5277, 407-824-3000; www.disneyworld.disney.go.com; 4401 Floridian Way🚌Disney, ⛴Disney, 🚝Disney) has a buffet breakfast featuring Winnie-the-Pooh, Mary Poppins and Alice in Wonderland, plus it holds the **Perfectly Princess Tea Party**. There's a jam-packed breakfast and dinner with Goofy, Donald Duck and pals at **Chef Mickey's** (p42) in **Disney's Contemporary Resort** (☎407-939-5277, 407-824-1000; www.disneyworld.disney.go.com; 4600 N World Dr; 🚌Disney, ⛴Disney, 🚝Disney); princesses mingle in Epcot's Norway at the **Akershus Royal Banquet** (p52); and the 100 Acre Wood folk come to Magic Kingdom's **Crystal Palace** for three meals a day.

Character Spots Each Walt Disney World® theme park has specific spots where Disney characters hang out, and you can simply hop in line (and wait and wait) to meet them and have your photo taken. A few character spots, such as **Enchanted Tales with Belle** (p25), include a short performance. In addition, check your map and Times Guide for times and locations of scheduled character greetings, and always keep your eyes open – you never know who you'll see!

Cinderella's Royal Table (p43) Cinderella greets guests and sits for a formal portrait (included in the price), and a sit-down meal with princesses is served upstairs. This is the only opportunity to eat inside the iconic castle – make reservations six months in advance. Hours vary.

Chip 'n' Dale Campfire Singalong (p55) A campfire singalong at Disney's Fort Wilderness Resort.

Martin Luther King Jr Day Third Monday in January

Presidents' Day Third Monday in February

Memorial Day Last Monday in May

Independence Day July 4

Labor Day First Monday in September

Columbus Day Second Monday in October

Veterans' Day November 11

Thanksgiving Fourth Thursday in November

Christmas Day December 25

Telephone Services

US country code ☏1

Orlando area code ☏407

Making international calls Dial ☏011 + country code + area code + local number.

Calling other US area codes or Canada Dial ☏1 + area code + seven-digit local number.

Calling within Orlando Just dial the seven-digit local number.

Cell phones

Most US cell phones – aside from iPhones – operate on CDMA, not the European standard of GSM. Be sure to double check compatibility with your phone service provider. Buying a cheap phone and loading it with prepaid minutes can often be cheaper than roaming charges.

Tourist Information

For on-site questions and reservations, head to Guest Services, just inside each theme park, or the concierge at any Disney resort hotel.

Official Visitor Center (Map p80; ☏407-363-5872; www.visitorlando.com; 8723 International Dr; ◷8:30am-6pm; ☐I-Ride Trolley Red Line 15) The best source for information on theme parks, accommodation,

Disney Numbers

Walt Disney World® (☏407-939-5277) Central number for all things Disney, including packages, tickets, room and dining reservations, and general questions about hours and scheduled events.

Walt Disney World® 'Disney Dining' (☏407-939-3463) Book priority dining reservations up to 180 days in advance, including character meals, dinner shows and specialty dining.

Walt Disney World® 'Enchanting Extras Collection' (Recreation) (☏407-939-7529) Horseback riding, boating and more.

Walt Disney World® 'Enchanting Extras Collection' (Tours) (☏407-939-8687) Tours at all of Disney's four theme parks.

Walt Disney World® 'Theme Parks Lost & Found' (☏407-824-4245) Items are sent to this central location at the end of each day.

outdoor activities, performing arts and more.

Orlando Informer (www.orlandoinformer.com) Excellent and detailed information on all things Universal, including park changes, money-saving tips, menus and a crowd calendar.

Universal Orlando Resort (www.universalorlando.com) Official site for information, accommodation and tickets.

Travelers with Disabilities

➡ Accommodation in Florida is required by law to offer wheelchair-accessible rooms. For questions about specialty rooms at Walt Disney World® Resort call ☎407-939-7807.

➡ Parks allow guests with special needs to avoid waiting in line, but do not offer front-of-the-line access. Disney issues a Disability Access Service card and Universal Orlando Resort issues the Attraction Assistance Pass (AAP). Guests take the card to the attraction they want to experience and they are given a return time based on current wait times. Both are available at Guest Services inside the park.

➡ Wheelchair and electric convenience vehicle (ECV) rental is at Guest Services at Walt Disney World® Resort, Universal Orlando Resort and SeaWorld theme parks.

➡ Go to individual park websites or Guest Services for details on accessibility, services for guests with cognitive disabilities, services for guests who are deaf or have hearing impairments, and services for guests who are visually impaired. Sign-language interpreting services require advanced reservations.

➡ Autism at the Parks (www.autismattheparks.com) provides comprehensive information on visiting Orlando theme parks with someone on the autism spectrum.

Universal Orlando Numbers

Universal Orlando Resort (☎407-363-8000, toll-free 800-232-7827) Central number for all things Universal (although it's infuriatingly automated).

Resort Hotel Reservations (☎888-273-1311, for vacation packages 888-343-3636) Accommodation at Universal's five on-site resort hotels.

Dining CityWalk & Theme Parks (☎407-224-9255) Advanced priority seating for CityWalk, Islands of Adventure and Universal Studios.

Dining Resort Hotels (☎407-503-3463) Advanced priority seating for Loews Portofino Bay, Hard Rock and Loews Royal Pacific Resorts.

Universal Orlando Resort Lost & Found (☎407-224-4233) Located inside Guest Services.

Guest Services (☎407-224-6350, 407-224-4233)

Visas

The Visa Waiver Program (VWP) allows visitors from Canada, the UK, Australia, New Zealand, Japan and many EU countries to enter the US without a visa for stays of less than 90 days.

If you are a citizen of a VWP country, you do not need a visa if you have a passport that meets current US standards *and* you have gotten approval from the Electronic System for Travel Authorization (ESTA) in advance. Register online with the Department of Homeland Security at https://esta.cbp.dhs.gov/esta at least 72 hours before arrival; once travel authorization is approved, your registration is valid for two years. The fee, payable online, is $14.

Those who need a visa – ie anyone staying longer than 90 days or from a non-VWP country – should see http://travel.state.gov.

Behind the Scenes

Send Us Your Feedback

We love to hear from travelers – your comments help make our books better. We read every word, and we guarantee that your feedback goes straight to the authors. Visit **lonelyplanet.com/contact** to submit your updates and suggestions.

Note: We may edit, reproduce and incorporate your comments in Lonely Planet products such as guidebooks, websites and digital products, so let us know if you don't want your comments reproduced or your name acknowledged. For a copy of our privacy policy visit lonelyplanet.com/privacy.

Kate's Thanks

La'Vell Brown: thank you for your magic wand, plus your passion, knowledge and insights of Disney World, and for transforming me from the Beastess into Cinderella herself. Thanks to Cory O'Born, Visit Orlando; Nathalia Romano and Ashlynn Webb, Universal Orlando; Jessica Savage, Greater Fort Lauderdale Convention & Visitors Bureau; and to Chris, for your flexibility, patience and everything (except holding my hand on the Hogwarts Express). Finally, thank you to Lauren Keith and Trisha Ping for their understanding and helping to put out a few nothing-but-Disney fireworks.

Acknowledgments

Climate map data adapted from Peel MC, Finlayson BL & McMahon TA (2007) 'Updated World Map of the Köppen-Geiger Climate Classification', Hydrology and Earth System Sciences, 11, 163344.
Cover photograph: Magic Kingdom, Walt Disney World® Resort, Peter Ptschelinzew/ Getty ©

This Book

This 2nd edition of Lonely Planet's *Pocket Orlando & Walt Disney World® Resort* guidebook was researched and written by Kate Armstrong. The previous edition was written by Jennifer Rasin Denniston. This guidebook was produced by the following:

Curator Kate Chapman

Destination Editors Lauren Keith, Trisha Ping

Product Editors Will Allen, Kate James

Regional Senior Cartographer Alison Lyall

Cartographer Julie Dodkins

Book Designer Jessica Rose

Assisting Book Designer Meri Blazevski

Assisting Editors Katie Connolly, Melanie Dankel

Cover Researcher Marika Mercer

Thanks to Cat Naghten, Sandie Kestell, Lauren O'Connell, Katie Penn, Tony Wheeler

Index

See also separate subindexes for:

⊗ **Eating p157**

⊙ **Drinking p158**

⊙ **Entertainment p158**

⊙ **Shopping p158**

⊗ Eating

Our Writer

Kate Armstrong

Kate Armstrong has spent much of her adult life traveling and living around the world. A full-time freelance travel journalist, she has contributed to around 40 Lonely Planet guides and trade publications and is regularly published in Australian and worldwide publications. She is the author of several books and children's educational titles. A keen photographer, greedy gourmand and frenetic festival goer, she enjoys exploring off-the-beaten-track locations, restaurants and theaters.

Published by Lonely Planet Global Limited
CRN 554153
2nd edition – Jan 2018
ISBN 978 1 78657 262 2
© Lonely Planet 2018 Photographs © as indicated 2018
10 9 8 7 6 5 4 3 2 1
Printed in Malaysia